Poems for
Grandmothers

This 2009 edition published by Barnes & Noble, Inc., by arrangement with Star Fire

STAR FIRE BOOKS
Crabtree Hall, Crabtree Lane
Fulham, London SW6 6TY
United Kingdom
www.star-fire.co.uk

Star Fire is part of The Foundry Creative Media Company Limited

Publisher and Creative Director: Nick Wells
Project Editor and Selection: Victoria Lyle
Designer: Theresa Maynard

Barnes & Noble, Inc.
122 Fifith Avenue
New York, NY 10011

ISBN 978-1-4351-1055-7

Printed in China

1 3 5 7 9 10 8 6 4 2

Every effort has been made to contact copyright holders. We apologize in advance for any
omissions and would be pleased to insert the appropriate acknowledgement in subsequent
editions of this publication.

While every endeavour has been made to ensure the accuracy of the reproduction on the
images in this book, we would be grateful to receive any comments or suggestions for
inclusion in future reprints.

Thanks to: Catherine Emslie, Victoria Garrard,
Chris Herbert, Rebecca Kidd and Sara Robson

Poems for
Grandmothers

Victoria Lyle

STAR FIRE BOOKS

Contents

Introduction

Grandmothers are important and integral members of the family. As it is said, they have all the fun and none of the responsibility. They also often have the time to devote to their children's children. They can therefore simply enjoy being with and caring for their grandchildren, unconcerned about being silly or spoiling them. This does not mean that they do not wish to teach them, whether that is behaviour or about the past. Including poems by William Shakespeare, Christina Georgina Rossetti and Lord Alfred Tennyson, this anthology explores the unique and multi-faceted role that grandmothers play.

The first chapter, 'The Family Tree', explores the relationships that tie a family together, particularly the reciprocal love between grandmothers and grandchildren. Grandmothers also make us aware of the generations of our

family that have preceded us and of our place in a web of individuals and relationships. There are poems that imagine an ancestor the poet has never known, but feels tied or indebted to in some way.

Visiting grandmothers and helping them around the house form happy and cherished memories. Cooking and cleaning seem far more fun when assisting grandma. 'Home Sweet Home' is a collection of poems reminiscing about such times. They also express gratitude for the work that grandmothers continue to do for their family.

'Fun and Games' celebrates the marvellous or ridiculous stories grandmothers tell, the rhymes they recite and the games they play. Grandmothers and grandchildren seem to share the same limitless imagination that turns the everyday

into the extraordinary; for example, a painted butterfly on a porridge bowl coming alive in 'Butterfly Laughter'.

Grandmothers have much life experience that they are keen to pass on to their loved ones. 'Wisdom and Teaching' is a selection of poems inspired by this knowledge. This encompasses many things, from washing hands to respecting nature. Grandmothers are not afraid to discipline the children in their care. 'Meddlesome Matty' and 'Opportunity' relate the tales of naughty children who think they can get away with misbehaving, but, of course, they cannot.

Grandmothers are also keen to impart their recollections of a life well lived. In 'Memories' stories from school, to romance, to the birth of children are related. Lord Alfred Tennyson's poem 'The Grandmother' is one characterful woman's story of life's pleasures and pains told to her granddaughter. The personal pleasure memories bring to an individual is also explored.

'The Passage of Time' acknowledges the aging process in a humorous and philosophical way. Many poems argue that, as Martin Farquhar Tupper writes, 'old as I seem, / My heart is full of youth'. Including William Shakespeare's famous poem 'All the World's a Stage' this chapter celebrates life in all its forms and at every age.

Grandmothers are influential and beloved figures and many poets have been inspired by their grandmothers or grandchildren. This anthology of poems celebrates these roles and relationships.

THE FAMILY TREE

A Grandmother Just Like You

I just want to let you know
You mean the world to me
Only a heart as dear as yours
Would give so unselfishly

The many things you've done
All the times you were there
Help me know deep down inside
How much you really care

Even though I might not say
I appreciate all you do
Richly blessed is how I feel
Having a grandmother just like you

Author Unknown

Grandmother

What could be more precious
than Grandma's special love?
She always seems to know the things
That we are fondest of.
She's always ready with a smile
Or a loving word of praise,
Her laughter always brightens up
The cloudiest of days...
She has an understanding heart
that encourages and cheers.
The love she gives so freely
Grows deeper with the years.
Her wisdom and devotion
are blessings from above –
Nothing could be more precious
than Grandma's special love.

Author Unknown

God Thought of All the Lovely Things

God thought of all the lovely things
She'd do to make life fun,
And she created Grandma
To be loved by everyone.

Author Unknown

Grandma

Grace and thoughtfulness shine through
Radiantly in all you do.
Acclaimed for the advice you share,
No one gives such love and care.
Dearly loved you'll always be,
Maker of sweet memories
Admired by all your family.

Author Unknown

And Grandma's Too

While we honour all our mothers
with words of love and praise.
While we tell about their goodness
and their kind and loving ways.
We should also think of Grandma,
she's a mother too, you see.
For she mothered my dear mother
as my mother mothers me.

Author Unknown

Mothers of Our Mother

Mothers of our mother,
Foremothers strong,
Guide our hands in yours,
Remind us how
To kindle the hearth.

Celtic blessing

Sonnet Three

Look in thy glass, and tell the face thou viewest
Now is the time that face should form another,
Whose fresh repair if now thou not renewest
Thou dost beguile the world, unbless some mother.
For where is she so fair whose unear'd womb
Disdains the tillage of thy husbandry?
Or who is he so fond will be the tomb
Of his self-love to stop posterity?
Thou art thy mother's glass, and she in thee
Calls back the lovely April of her prime;
So thou through windows of thine age shall see
Despite of wrinkles this thy golden time.
    But if thou live remember'd not to be,
    Die single, and thine image dies with thee.

William Shakespeare (1564–1616)

Written Upon Receiving a New Year's Gift

I have a little Grandchild dear,
Who sends to me on each new year
   A valuable present:
Not costly gift from store-house bought,
But one that her own hands have wrought,
   Therefore to me more pleasant.

Accept, dear child, the wish sincere,
For you much happiness this year,
   And length of days be given;
Here may you act well your part,
Serving the Lord with all your heart,
   And find your rest in heaven.

Mary Ann H.T. Bigelow (d. 1870)

Extract from For My Grand-Daughters

Mary and Lily – how sweet are those names,
Allied as they are to my heart and my home;
Recalling with freshness the days that are past,
Yielding buds of sweet promise for days yet to come.
Links are these names to the chain that hath bound
In fetters my heart, to which still they lay claim;
Loved ones and lovely, still close by me found,
Years past, and time present, whose names are the same.

Mary Ann H.T. Bigelow (d. 1870)

The Great Grandfather

My father's grandfather lives still,
    His age is fourscore years and ten;
He looks a monument of time,
    The agedest of aged men.

Though years lie on him like a load,
    A happier man you will not see
Than he, whenever he can get
    His great grandchildren on his knee.

When we our parents have displeased,
    He stands between us as a screen;
By him our good deeds in the sun,
    Our bad ones in the shade are seen.

His love's a line that's long drawn out,
    Yet lasteth firm unto the end;
His heart is oak, yet unto us
    It like the gentlest reed can bend.

A fighting soldier he has been –
   Yet by his manners you would guess,
That he his whole long life had spent
   In scenes of country quietness.

His talk is all of things long past,
   For modern facts no pleasure yield –
Of the famed year of forty-five,
   Of William, and Culloden's field.

The deeds of this eventful age,
   Which princes from their thrones have hurled,
Can no more interest wake in him
   Than stories of another world.

When I his length of days revolve,
   How like a strong tree he hath stood,
It brings into my mind almost
   Those patriarchs old before the flood.

Charles Lamb (1775–1834)

The Grandfather's Departure

The Old Man press'd Palemon's hand;
   To Lucy nodded with a smile;
Kiss'd all the little ones around;
   Then clos'd the gate, and paus'd awhile.

'When shall I come again!' he thought,
   Ere yet the journey had begun;
It was a tedious length of way,
   But he beheld an only son.

And dearly did he love to take
　　A rosy grandchild on his knee;
To part his shining locks, and say,
　　'Just such another boy was he!'

And never felt he greater pride,
　　And never did he look so gay,
As when the little urchins strove
　　To make him partner in their play.

But when, in some more gentle mood,
　　They silent hung upon his arm,
Or nestled close at ev'ning pray'r,
　　The old man felt a softer charm;

And upward rais'd his closing eye,
　　Whence slow effus'd a grateful tear,
As if his senses own'd a joy,
　　Too holy for endurance here.

No heart e'er pray'd so fervently,
　　Unprompted by an earthly zeal,
None ever knew such tenderness,
　　That did not true devotion feel.

As with the pure, uncolour'd flame,
　　The violet's richest blues unite,
Do our affections soar to heav'n,
　　And rarify and beam with light.

Matilda Betham (1776–1852)

My Mother

Who sat and watched my infant head
When sleeping on my cradle bed,
And tears of sweet affection shed?
My Mother.

When pain and sickness made me cry,
Who gazed upon my heavy eye,
And wept for fear that I should die?
My Mother.

Who taught my infant lips to pray
And love God's holy book and day,
And walk in wisdom's pleasant way?
My Mother.

And can I ever cease to be
Affectionate and kind to thee,
Who wast so very kind to me,
My Mother?

Ah, no! The thought I cannot bear,
And if God please my life to spare
I hope I shall reward they care,
My Mother.

When thou art feeble, old and grey,
My healthy arm shall be thy stay,
And I will soothe thy pains away,
My Mother.

Ann Taylor (1782–1866)

The Mother's Heart

I
When first thou camest, gentle, shy, and fond,
My eldest-born, first hope, and dearest treasure,
My heart received thee with a joy beyond
All that it yet had felt of earthly pleasure;
Nor thought that any love again might be
So deep and strong as that I felt for thee.

II
Faithful and true, with sense beyond thy years,
And natural piety that lean'd to Heaven;
Wrung by a harsh word suddenly to tears,
Yet patient of rebuke when justly given,
Obedient, easy to be reconciled,
And meekly-cheerful – such wert thou, my child!

III
Not willing to be left; still by my side
Haunting my walks, while summer-day was dying;
Nor leaving in thy turn; but pleased to glide
Thro' the dark room where I was sadly lying,
Or by the couch of pain, a sitter meek,
Watch the dim eye, and kiss the feverish cheek.

IV

O boy! Of such as thou are oftenest made
Earth's fragile idols; like a tender flower,
No strength in all thy freshness, prone to fade,
And bending weakly to the thunder-shower,
Still, round the loved, thy heart found force to bind,
And clung, like woodbine shaken in the wind!

V

Then THOU, my merry love; bold in thy glee,
Under the bough, or by the firelight dancing,
With thy sweet temper, and thy spirit free,
Didst come, as restless as a bird's wing glancing,
Full of a wild and irrepressible mirth,
Like a young sunbeam to the gladden'd earth!

VI

Thine was the shout! The song! The burst of joy!
Which sweet from childhood's rosy lip resoundeth;
Thine was the eager spirit nought could cloy,
And the glad heart from which all grief reboundeth;
And many a mirthful jest and mock reply,
Lurk'd in the laughter of thy dark-blue eye!

VII

And thine was many an art to win and bless,
The cold and stern to joy and fondness warming;
The coaxing smile; the frequent soft caress;
The earnest tearful prayer all wrath disarming!
Again my heart a new affection found,
But thought that lore with thee had reach'd its bound.

VIII

At length THOU camest; thou, the last and least;
Nick-named 'The Emperor' by thy laughing brothers,
Because a haughty spirit swell'd thy breast,
And thou didst seek to rule and sway the others;
Mingling with every playful infant wile
A mimic majesty that made us smile:

IX

And oh! Most like a regal child wert thou!
An eye of resolute and successful scheming!
Fair shoulders, curling lip, and dauntless brow,
Fit for the world's strife, not for Poet's dreaming:
And proud the lifting of thy stately head,
And the firm bearing of thy conscious tread.

X

Different from both! Yet each succeeding claim,
I, that all other love had been forswearing,
Forthwith admitted, equal and the same;
Nor injured either, by this love's comparing,
Nor stole a fraction for the newer call –
But in the Mother's heart, found room for ALL!

Caroline Elizabeth Sarah Norton (1808–77)

Verses Added to the Foregoing
By the Baby's Paternal Grandmother

Unconscious babe! Not even lines like these
Have power thy little slumbering sense to please,
Nor all the charms portrayed with so much grace,
Can force one smile from that soft 'placid face.'
But oh, how sweetly on the parents' ear
Fall tender tones of love from one so dear!
How seems the little form that pen has traced,
With future charms and virtues to be graced,
While brighter seem the hopes such love bestows,
And the fair prospect with fresh beauty glows.
Dear, dear Joanna, well employed art thou
In weaving chaplets for this baby's brow!
For this dear babe, who had so welcome been
To those who now on earth no more are seen!
For me, for me, in these declining days,
Nothing remains but humble prayer and praise:
Praise for the precious boon already given,
Prayers for its endless happiness in Heaven!

Joanna Baillie (1762–1851)

Dorothy Q.

Grandmother's mother: her age, I guess,
Thirteen summers, or something less;
Girlish bust, but womanly air;
Smooth, square forehead with uprolled hair;
Lips that lover has never kissed;
Taper fingers and slender wrist;
Hanging sleeves of stiff brocade;
So they painted the little maid.

On her hand a parrot green
Sits unmoving and broods serene.
Hold up the canvas full in view –
Look! There's a rent the light shines through,
Dark with a century's fringe of dust –
That was a Red-Coat's rapier-thrust!
Such is the tale the lady old,
Dorothy's daughter's daughter, told.

Who the painter was none may tell –
One whose best was not over well;
Hard and dry, it must be confessed,
Fist as a rose that has long been pressed;
Yet in her cheek the hues are bright,
Dainty colors of red and white,
And in her slender shape are seen
Hint and promise of stately mien.

Look not on her with eyes of scorn –
Dorothy Q. was a lady born!
Ay! Since the galloping Normans came,
England's annals have known her name;
And still to the three-hilled rebel town
Dear is that ancient name's renown,
For many a civic wreath they won,
The youthful sire and the gray-haired son.

O Damsel Dorothy! Dorothy Q.!
Strange is the gift that I owe to you;
Such a gift as never a king
Save to daughter or son might bring –
All my tenure of heart and hand,
All my title to house and land;
Mother and sister and child and wife
And joy and sorrow and death and life!
What if a hundred years ago
Those close-shut lips had answered NO,
When forth the tremulous question came
That cost the maiden her Norman name,
And under the folds that look so still
The bodice swelled with the bosom's thrill?
Should I be I, or would it be
One tenth another, to nine tenths me?

Soft is the breath of a maiden's YES:
Not the light gossamer stirs with less;
But never a cable that holds so fast
Through all the battles of wave and blast,
And never an echo of speech or song
That lives in the babbling air so long!
There were tones in the voice that whispered then
You may hear to-day in a hundred men.

O lady and lover, how faint and far
Your images hover – and here we are,
Solid and stirring in flesh and bone –
Edward's and Dorothy's, all their own –
A goodly record for Time to show
Of a syllable spoken so long ago!
Shall I bless you, Dorothy, or forgive
For the tender whisper that bade me live?

It shall be a blessing, my little maid!
I will heal the stab of the Red-Coat's blade,
And freshen the gold of the tarnished frame,
And gild with a rhyme your household name;
So you shall smile on us brave and bright
As first you greeted the morning's light,
And live untroubled by woes and fears
Through a second youth of a hundred years.

Oliver Wendell Holmes Snr (1809–94)

Baby

Where did you come from, baby dear?
Out of the everywhere into here.

Where did you get those eyes so blue?
Out of the sky as I came through.

What makes the light in them sparkle and spin?
Some of the starry twinkles left in.

Where did you get that little tear?
I found it waiting when I got here.

What makes your forehead so smooth and high?
A soft hand stroked it as I went by.

What makes your cheek like a warm white rose?
I saw something better than any one knows.

Whence that three-cornered smile of bliss?
Three angels gave me at once a kiss.

Where did you get this pearly ear?
God spoke, and it came out to hear.

Where did you get those arms and hands?
Love made itself into bonds and bands.

Feet, whence did you come, you darling things?
From the same box as the cherubs' wings.

How did they all just come to be you?
God thought about me, and so I grew.

But how did you come to us, you dear?
God thought about you, and so I am here.

George MacDonald (1824–1905)

Thank God for Little Children

Thank God for little children,
Bright flowers by earth's wayside,
The dancing, joyous lifeboats
Upon life's stormy tide.

Thank God for little children;
When our skies are cold and gray,
They come as sunshine to our hearts,
And charm our cares away.

I almost think the angels,
Who tend life's garden fair,
Drop down the sweet wild blossoms
That bloom around us here.

It seems a breath of heaven
Round many a cradle lies,
And every little baby
Brings a message from the skies.

Dear mothers, guard these jewels.
As sacred offerings meet,
A wealth of household treasures
To lay at Jesus' feet.

Frances Ellen Watkins (1825–1911)

I Know a Baby, Such a Baby

I know a baby, such a baby,
Round blue eyes and cheeks of pink,
Such an elbow furrowed with dimples,
Such a wrist where creases sink.
'Cuddle and love me, cuddle and love me,'
Crows the mouth of coral pink:
Oh, the bald head, and, oh, the sweet lips,
And, oh, the sleepy eyes that wink!

Christina Georgina Rossetti (1830–94)

The Peach Tree on the Southern Wall

The peach tree on the southern wall
Has basked so long beneath the sun,
Her score of peaches great and small
Bloom rosy, every one.
A peach for brothers, one for each,
A peach for you and a peach for me;
But the biggest, rosiest, downiest peach
For Grandmamma with her tea.

Christina Georgina Rossetti (1830–94)

Harry the First

In his arm-chair, warmly cushioned,
In the quiet earned by labor,
Life's reposeful Indian summer,
Grandpa sits; and lets the paper
Lie upon his knee unheeded.
Shine his cheeks like winter apples,
Gleams his smile like autumn sunshine,
As he looks on little Harry,
First-born of the house of Graham,
Bravely cutting teeth in silence,
Cutting teeth with looks heroic.
Some deep thought seems moving Grandpa,
Ponders he awhile in silence,
Then he turns, and says to Grandma,
'Nancy, do you think that ever
There was such a child before?'

Grandma, with prim precision
The seam-stitch impaleth deftly
On her sharp and glittering needle,
Then she turns and answers calmly,
With a deep assurance – 'Never
Was there such a child before!'

Papa thinks so, but in manly
Dignity controls his feelings;
More than half a year a father,

He must show a cool composure,
He must stately be if ever.
But his dark eyes plainly tell it,
Tell it, as he sayeth proudly,
'Papa's man is little Harry.'

Mamma, maybe, does not speak it,
But she prints the thought on velvet,
Rosy-hued, with fondest kisses,
When the pink, soft page is lying
Folded closely to her bosom.

A little farther goes his auntie,
Aged fourteen, age of fancy;
She looks down the future ages
With her wise, prophetic vision;
Sees the babies pass before her,
Babies of the twentieth century,
All the long and dusty ages,
To the thousand years of glory.
Oh, the host of bright-eyed children,
Thronging like the stars at midnight,
Faces sweet and countless, as the
Rose-leaves of a thousand summers.
All the pretty heads so curly
That shall hold a riper wisdom
Than our youthful planet dreams of;
All the ranks of dimple shoulders,
That shall move Time's rolling chariot

Nearer to the golden city;
Vieweth these the blue-eyed prophet,
Still the oracle says calmly,
Speaks the seer with golden tresses –
'No! There never was, nor will be
Such a child as our Harry,
Such a noble boy as Harry.'

Summer brings a wealth of flowers,
Flowers of every form and colour,
Orange, crimson, royal purple,
All along the mountain passes,
All along the pleasant valley,
Low the emerald branches bendeth
With their weight of summer glory.

But they do not waken in us
Half the tender, blissful feeling,
Half the pure and sweet emotion
As the first spring-flower in April,
With its lashes tinged with crimson,
Partly raised from eyes half-timid,
Fearful that the snow will drown it;
How we love the dainty blossom,
How we wear it in our bosom.

Just so with the tree ancestral,
Many flowers may blossom on it,
But the first wee bud that's grafted,
To its heart, ah, how we love it;
Others may be loved as fondly,
But they are not loved so proudly,
Loved so blindly, so entirely.
Yes, when first the heart's door opens
To the touch of baby fingers,
Quick the dimpled feet will bear them
To the dearest place and warmest
Plenty room enough for other
Buds of beauty, buds of promise,
In the heart's capacious chambers;
But the first is firmly settled –
Little Harry's firmly settled
In the centre of affection;
Later ones must settle round him.

Marietta Holley (1836–1926)

My Mother's Love

My vision eye beholds a form,
Bent low by years of life's fierce storm,
    That moves with feeble tread;
Though time has worn that weary frame
The heart still keeps its sacred flame
    True, undiminished.

No power but Death can ever quell –
No mortal tongue can ever tell
    A mother's boundless love;
'Tis shadowed in the secret sigh,
Or in the moisture of the eye –
    E'en silence, it may prove.

Itself and I had but one birth,
It came from heaven to gladden earth –
    And brighten man's abode;
To feel the magic of its power
Is richer boon than any dower
    The earth has yet bestowed.

Favoured in this has been my lot;
Relentless Death has robbed me not –
    Though fifty years have flown,
Of all the ecstasy and joy
That came to me when but a boy,
    Or since to manhood grown,

Of that benign maternal smile,
Whose magic influence can beguile
   My heart from worldly care,
And lead me toward that beacon-light
Of motive pure and act aright,
   No matter when or where.

O blessed influence of the past!
May all my mother's counsels last
   Until my heart shall cease
To send its crimson current round
The tenement wherein 'tis bound,
   And Death shall bring release.

Still let these visions come to me
Of her I would so gladly see
   Though far from her I roam;
They bring sweet memory of the past,
Which but a few more years may last,
   Of happiness and home.

Jared Barhite (1840–1921)

The Golden Wedding of Sterling and Sarah Lanier
By the Eldest Grandson

A rainbow span of fifty years,
Painted upon a cloud of tears,
In blue for hopes and red for fears,
    Finds end in a golden hour to-day.
Ah, YOU to our childhood the legend told,
'At the end of the rainbow lies the gold,'
And now in our thrilling hearts we hold
    The gold that never will pass away.

Gold crushed from the quartz of a crystal life,
Gold hammered with blows of human strife,
Gold burnt in the love of man and wife,
    Till it is pure as the very flame:
Gold that the miser will not have,
Gold that is good beyond the grave,
Gold that the patient and the brave
    Amass, neglecting praise and blame.

O golden hour that caps the time
Since, heart to heart like rhyme to rhyme,
You stood and listened to the chime
    Of inner bells by spirits rung,
That tinkled many a secret sweet
Concerning how two souls should meet,
And whispered of Time's flying feet
With a most piquant silver tongue.

O golden day, a golden crown
For the kingly heads that bowed not down
To win a smile or 'scape a frown,
    Except the smile and frown of Heaven!
Dear heads, still dark with raven hair;
Dear hearts, still white in spite of care;
Dear eyes, still black and bright and fair
    As any eyes to mortals given!

Old parents of a restless race,
You miss full many a bonny face
That would have smiled a filial grace
    Around your Golden Wedding wine.
But God is good and God is great.
His will be done, if soon or late.
Your dead stand happy in yon Gate
    And call you blessed while they shine.

So, drop the tear and dry the eyes.
Your rainbow glitters in the skies.
Here's golden wine: young, old, arise:
    With cups as full as our souls, we say:
'Two Hearts, that wrought with smiles through tears
This rainbow span of fifty years,
Behold how true, true love appears
    True gold for your Golden Wedding day!'

Sidney Lanier (1842–81)

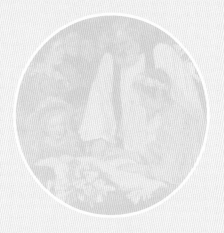

Personally Addressed
Written for a Golden Wedding

Just fifty years ago to-night,
    When earth was mantled deep with snow,
The stars beheld with tender light
    The fairest scene this world can show.

Two graceful forms stood side by side,
    Two trembling hands were clasped as one,
Two hearts exchanged perpetual faith,
    And love's sweet poem was begun.

For suns may rise and suns may set,
    And tides may ebb and tides may flow,
Love is man's greatest blessing yet,
    And honest wedlock makes it so.

'Father' and 'Mother' – sweetest words
    That human lips can ever frame,
We gather here as children now
    To find your loving hearts the same.

Unchanged, unchangeable by time,
    Your love is boundless as the sea;
The same as when our childish griefs
    Were hushed beside our mother's knee.

Years may have given us separate homes,
    Friends, children, happiness and fame,
But oh! To-night our greatest wealth
    Is that we call you still by name.

God bless you both! For fifty years
    You've journeyed onward side by side;
And still, for years to come, God grant
    Your paths may nevermore divide;

But, just as sunset's golden glow
    Makes Alpine snows divinely fair,
So may the setting sun of life
    Rest lightly on your silvered hair!

Yes, suns may rise and suns may set,
    And tides may ebb and tides may flow,
We are your loving children yet,
    And time will ever prove us so.

John Lawson Stoddard (1850–1931)

To Dick, on His Sixth Birthday

Tho' I am very old and wise,
And you are neither wise nor old,
When I look far into your eyes,
I know things I was never told:
I know how flame must strain and fret
Prisoned in a mortal net;
How joy with over-eager wings,
Bruises the small heart where he sings;
How too much life, like too much gold,
Is sometimes very hard to hold…
All that is talking – I know
This much is true, six years ago
An angel living near the moon
Walked thru the sky and sang a tune
Plucking stars to make his crown –
And suddenly two stars fell down,
Two falling arrows made of light.
Six years ago this very night
I saw them fall and wondered why
The angel dropped them from the sky –
But when I saw your eyes I knew
The angel sent the stars to you.

Sara Teasdale (1884–1933)

The Cross-Current

Through twelve stout generations
New England blood I boast;
The stubborn pastures bred them,
The grim, uncordial coast,

Sedate and proud old cities,
Loved well enough by me,
Then how should I be yearning
To scour the earth and sea.

Each of my Yankee forbears
Wed a New England mate:
They dwelt and did and died here,
Nor glimpsed a rosier fate.

My clan endured their kindred;
But foreigners they loathed,
And wandering folk, and minstrels,
And gypsies motley-clothed.

Then why do patches please me,
Fantastic, wild array?
Why have I vagrant fancies
For lads from far away.

My folk were godly Churchmen,
Or paced in Elders' weeds;
But all were grave and pious
And hated heathen creeds.

Then why are Thor and Wotan
To dread forces still?
Why does my heart go questing
For Pan beyond the hill?

My people clutched at freedom.
Though others' wills they chained,
But made the Law and kept it,
And Beauty, they restrained.

Then why am I a rebel
To laws of rule and square?
Why would I dream and dally,
Or, reckless, do and dare?

O righteous, solemn Grandsires,
O dames, correct and mild,
Who bred me of your virtues!
Whence comes this changing child?

The thirteenth generation,
Unlucky number this!
My grandma loved a Pirate,
And all my faults are his!

A gallant, ruffled rover,
With beauty-loving eye,
He swept Colonial waters
Of coarser, bloodier fry.

He waved his hat to danger,
At Law he shook his fist.
Ah, merrily he plundered,
He sang and fought and kissed!

Though none have found his treasure,
And none his part would take,
I bless that thirteenth lady
Who chose him for my sake!

Abbie Farwell Brown (1875–1927)

In Grandma's Lap

A truly special place
of safety, of security,
of love, nestled in
Grandma's lap she lay
warm and secure,
feeling love, contentment,
in Grandma's lap.

Raymond A. Foss (b.1960)

HOME SWEET HOME

Washing-Day

The Muses are turned gossips; they have lost
The buskined step, and clear high-sounding phrase,
Language of gods. Come then, domestic Muse,
In slipshod measure loosely prattling on
Of farm or orchard, pleasant curds and cream,
Or drowning flies, or shoe lost in the mire
By little whimpering boy, with rueful face;
Come, Muse, and sing the dreaded Washing-Day.
Ye who beneath the yoke of wedlock bend,
With bowed soul, full well ye ken the day
Which week, smooth sliding after week, brings on
Too soon; for to that day nor peace belongs
Nor comfort; ere the first grey streak of dawn,
The red-armed washers come and chase repose.
Nor pleasant smile, nor quaint device of mirth,
E'er visited that day: the very cat,
From the wet kitchen scared and reeking hearth,
Visits the parlour, an unwonted guest.
The silent breakfast-meal is soon dispatched;
Uninterrupted, save by anxious looks
Cast at the lowering sky, if sky should lower.
From that last evil, O preserve us, heavens!
For should the skies pour down, adieu to all
Remains of quiet: then expect to hear
Of sad disasters, dirt and gravel stains
Hard to efface, and loaded lines at once
Snapped short, and linen-horse by dog thrown down,
And all the petty miseries of life.
Saints have been calm while stretched upon the rack,

And Guatimozin smiled on burning coals;
But never yet did housewife notable
Greet with a smile a rainy washing-day.
But grant the welkin fair, require not thou
Who call'st thyself perchance the master there,
Or study swept, or nicely dusted coat,
Or usual 'tendance; ask not, indiscreet,
Thy stockings mended, though the yawning rents
Gape wide as Erebus; nor hope to find
Some snug recess impervious: shouldst thou try
The 'customed garden walks, thine eye shall rue
The budding fragrance of thy tender shrubs,
Myrtle or rose, all crushed beneath the weight
Of coarse checked apron, with impatient hand
Twitched off when showers impend: or crossing lines
Shall mar thy musings, as the wet cold sheet
Flaps in thy face abrupt. Woe to the friend
Whose evil stars have urged him forth to claim
On such a day the hospitable rites!
Looks, blank at best, and stinted courtesy,
Shall he receive. Vainly he feeds his hopes
With dinner of roast chicken, savoury pie,
Or tart or pudding: pudding he nor tart
That day shall eat; nor, though the husband try,
Mending what can't be helped, to kindle mirth
From cheer deficient, shall his consort's brow
Clear up propitious: the unlucky guest
In silence dines, and early slinks away.
I well remember, when a child, the awe
This day struck into me; for then the maids,
I scarce knew why, looked cross, and drove me from them:

Nor soft caress could I obtain, nor hope
Usual indulgencies; jelly or creams,
Relic of costly suppers, and set by
For me their petted one; or buttered toast,
When butter was forbid; or thrilling tale
Of ghost or witch, or murder – so I went
And sheltered me beside the parlour fire:
There my dear grandmother, eldest of forms,
Tended the little ones, and watched from harm,
Anxiously fond, though oft her spectacles
With elfin cunning hid, and oft the pins
Drawn from her ravelled stocking, might have soured
One less indulgent.
At intervals my mother's voice was heard,
Urging dispatch: briskly the work went on,
All hands employed to wash, to rinse, to wring,
To fold, and starch, and clap, and iron, and plait.
Then would I sit me down, and ponder much
Why washings were. Sometimes through hollow bowl
Of pipe amused we blew, and sent aloft
The floating bubbles; little dreaming then
To see, Mongolfier, thy silken ball
Ride buoyant through the clouds – so near approach
The sports of children and the toils of men.
Earth, air, and sky, and ocean, hath its bubbles,
And verse is one of them – this most of all.

Anna Laetitia Aikin Barbauld (1743–1825)

Home, Sweet Home

Mid pleasures and palaces though we may roam,
Be it ever so humble, there's no place like home;
A charm from the sky seems to hallow us there,
Which, seek through the world, is ne'er met with elsewhere.
Home, home, sweet, sweet home!
There's no place like home, oh, there's no place like home!

An exile from home, splendor dazzles in vain;
Oh, give me my lowly thatched cottage again!
The birds singing gayly, that come at my call –
Give me them – and the peace of mind, dearer than all!
Home, home, sweet, sweet home!
There's no place like home, oh, there's no place like home!

I gaze on the moon as I tread the drear wild,
And feel that my mother now thinks of her child,
As she looks on that moon from our own cottage door
Thro' the woodbine, whose fragrance shall cheer me no more.
Home, home, sweet, sweet home!
There's no place like home, oh, there's no place like home!

How sweet 'tis to sit 'neath a fond father's smile,
And the caress of a mother to soothe and beguile!
Let others delight mid new pleasures to roam,
But give me, oh, give me, the pleasures of home.
Home, home, sweet, sweet home!
There's no place like home, oh, there's no place like home!

To thee I'll return, overburdened with care;
The heart's dearest solace will smile on me there;
No more from that cottage again will I roam;
Be it ever so humble, there's no place like home.
Home, home, sweet, sweet, home!
There's no place like home, oh, there's no place like home!

John Howard Payne (1791–1852)

Extract from Grandmother

Her cottage drowned in roses, sitting
Before it Grannam plies her knitting;
And, prosperous from their city life,
Her Grandson near sits with his wife.

Before them play their boy and girl,
So fair with many a tangled curl,
Tumbling about, with laughing shout,
As aye they find some floweret out.
A race! They come; with Grannie lies
To say who holds the richer prize.
Her glasses wiped, with solemn air
She ponders well, she judges fair.
Judgment pronounced, the little chap,
Back she lays him on her lap,
And measures nice if still her knitting
That stumpy leg be duly fitting.

Thomas Aird (1802–76)

The New-England Boy's Song About Thanksgiving Day

Over the river, and through the wood,
To grandfather's house we go;
The horse knows the way,
To carry the sleigh,
Through the white and drifted snow.

Over the river, and through the wood,
To grandfather's house away!
We would not stop
For doll or top,
For 't is Thanksgiving Day.

Over the river, and through the wood,
Oh, how the wind does blow!
It stings the toes,
And bites the nose,
As over the ground we go.

Over the river, and through the wood,
With a clear blue winter sky,
The dogs do bark,
And children hark,
As we go jingling by.

Over the river, and through the wood,
To have a first-rate play;
Hear the bells ring
Ting a ling ding,
Hurra for Thanksgiving Day!

Over the river, and through the wood,
No matter for winds that blow;
Or if we get
The sleigh upset,
Into a bank of snow.

Over the river, and through the wood,
To see little John and Ann;
We will kiss them all,
And play snow-ball,
And stay as long as we can.

Over the river, and through the wood,
Trot fast, my dapple grey!
Spring over the ground,
Like a hunting hound,
For 't is Thanksgiving Day!

Over the river, and through the wood,
And straight through the barn-yard gate;
We seem to go
Extremely slow,
It is so hard to wait.

Over the river, and through the wood,
Old Jowler hears our bells;
He shakes his pow,
With a loud bow wow,
And thus the news he tells.

Over the river, and through the wood,
When grandmother sees us come,
She will say, 'Oh dear,
The children are here,
Bring a pie for every one.'

Over the river, and through the wood,
Now grandmother's cap I spy!
Hurra for the fun!
Is the pudding done?
Hurra for the pumpkin pie!

Lydia Maria Francis Child (1802–80)

Grand'ther Baldwin's Thanksgiving

Underneath protected branches, from the highway just aloof;
Stands the house of Grand'ther Baldwin, with its gently sloping roof.

Square of shape and solid-timbered, it was standing, I have heard,
In the days of Whig and Tory, under royal George the Third.

Many a time, I well remember, I have gazed with Childish awe
At the bullet-hole remaining in the sturdy oaken door,

Turning round half-apprehensive (recking not how time had fled)
Of the lurking, savage foeman from whose musket it was sped.

Not far off, the barn, plethoric with the autumn's harvest spoils,
Holds the farmer's well-earned trophies – the guerdon of his toils;

Filled the lofts with hay, sweet-scented, ravished from the
    meadows green,
While beneath are stalled the cattle, with their quiet, drowsy mien.

Deep and spacious are the grain-bins, brimming o'er with
    nature's gold;
Here are piles of yellow pumpkins on the barn-floor loosely rolled.

Just below in deep recesses, safe from wintry frost chill,
There are heaps of ruddy apples from the orchard on the hill.

Many a year has Grand'ther Baldwin in the old house dwelt in peace,
As his hair each year grew whiter, he has seen his herds increase.

Sturdy sons and comely daughters, growing up from childish plays,
One by one have met life's duties, and gone forth their several ways.

Hushed the voice of childish laughter, hushed is childhood's
  merry tone,
the fireside Grand'ther Baldwin and his good wife sit alone.

Turning round half-apprehensive (recking not how time had fled)
Of the lurking savage foeman from whose musket it was sped.

Not far off, the barn, plethoric with the autumn harvest spoils,
Holds the farmer's well-earned trophies – the guerdon of his toils;

Filled the lofts with hay, sweet-scented, ravished from the
  meadows green,
While beneath are stalled the cattle, with their quiet drowsy mien.

Deep and spacious are the grain-bins, brimming o'er with
  nature's gold;
Here are piles of yellow pumpkins on the barn-floor loosely rolled.

Just below in deep recesses, safe from wintry frost and chill,
There are heaps of ruddy apples from the orchard on the hill.

Many a year has Grand'ther Baldwin in the old house dwelt in peace,
As his hair each year grew whiter, he has seen his herds increase.

Sturdy sons and comely daughters, growing up from childish plays,
One by one have met life's duties, and gone forth their several ways.

Hushed the voice of childish laughter, hushed is childhood's
    merry tone,
By the fireside Grand'ther Baldwin and his good wife sit alone.

Yet once within the twelvemonth, when the days are short and drear,
And chill winds chant the requiem of the slowly fading year,

When the autumn work is over, and the harvest gathered in,
Once again the old house echoes to a long unwonted din.

Logs of hickory blaze and crackle in the fireplace huge anti high,
Curling wreaths of smoke mount upward to the gray November sky.

Ruddy lads and smiling lasses, just let loose from schooldom's cares,
Patter, patter, race and clatter, up and down the great hall stairs.

All the boys shall hold high revel; all the girls shall have their way;
That's the law at Grand'ther Baldwin's upon each Thanksgiving Day.

From the parlor's sacred precincts, hark! A madder uproar yet;
Roguish Charlie's playing stage-coach, and the stage-coach has upset!

Joe, black-eyed and laughter-loving, Grand'ther's specs his
    nose across,
Gravely winks at brother Willie, who is gayly playing horse.

Grandma's face is fairly radiant; Grand'ther knows not how to frown,
though the children, in their frolic, turn the old house upside down.

For the boys may hold high revel, and the girls must have their way;
That's the law at Grand'ther Baldwin's upon each Thanksgiving Day.

But the dinner – ah! The dinner – words are feeble to portray
What a culinary triumph is achieved Thanksgiving Day!

Fairly groans the board with dainties, but the turkey rules the roast,
Aldermanic at the outset, at the last a fleshless ghost.

Then the richness of the pudding, and the flavour of the pie,
When you've dined at Grandma Baldwin's you will know as
    well as I.

When, at length, the feast was ended, Grand'ther Baldwin bent
    his head,
And, amid the solemn silence, with a reverent voice, he said:

'Now unto God, the Gracious One, we thanks and homage pay,
Who guardeth us, and guideth us, and loveth us always!

'He scatters blessings in our paths, He giveth us increase,
He crowns us with His kindnesses, and granteth us His peace.

'Unto himself, our wandering feet, we pray that He may draw,
And may we strive, with faithful hearts, to keep His holy law!'

His simple words in silence died: a moment's hush. And then
From all the listening hearts there rose a solemn-voiced 'Amen!'

Horatio Alger Jr (1832–99)

The Needle and Thread

The Needle and Thread one day were wed,
The Thimble acted as priest,
A paper of Pins, and the Scissors twins
Were among the guests at the feast.

That dandy trim the Bodkin slim
Danced with Miss Tape-measure,
But he stepped on her trail, and she called him
    'a whale,'
And that put an end to their pleasure.

Wrinkled and fat the Beeswax sat
And talked with the Needle-case.
'I am glad,' she said, 'that my niece, the Thread,
Has married into this race.

'Her mother, the Spool, was a dull old fool,
And the Needle and Thread were shy;
The result you see came all through me,
I taught her to catch his eye.'

The Emery-ball just there had a fall –
She had danced too long at one time,
And that put a stop to the merry hop,
And that brings an end to my rhyme.

The groom and the bride took their wedding ride
Down a long white-seam to the shore,
And the guests all said there never was wed
So fair a couple before.

Ella Wheeler Wilcox (1850–1919)

Going to See Grandmamma

Little Molly and Damon
   Are walking so far,
For they're going to see
   Their kind Grandmamma.

And they very well know,
   When they get there she'll take
From out of her cupboard
   Some very nice cake.

And into her garden
   They know they may run,
And pick some red currants,
   And have lots of fun.

So Damon to doggie
   Says, 'How do you do?'
And asks his mamma
   If he may not go too.

Kate Greenaway (1846–1901)

Extract from Knitting

My muse is in the sulks to-day,
I've tried in vain to find
A subject fit for rhyme and song,
Just suited to my mind.
I called last night upon the stars,
To-day upon the sun,
My muse would leave me in the lurch,
With just a line begun.
I tried to work, I tried to sing,
And then I tried to play;
And then I took my knitting up,
To while the time away.
And then the flashes of quick thought,
With bliss thrilled all my soul;
With every stitch did fancy's hand,
A saddening page unroll.
The dullest of the dullest work,
So tiresome, and so slow!
To knit, and knit, the live-long day,
And still small increase show.
But as I knit, a fairy web
My brain wore in its dreaming,
And in each stitch my fancy saw
Some bright poetic gleaming.

Mary Eliza Perine Tucker Lambert (1838–1938)

Extract from Granny

Here, in her elbow chair, she sits
    A soul alert, alive,
A poor old body shrunk and bent –
    The queen-bee of the hive.

But hives of bees and hives of men
    Obey their several laws;
No fiercely-loving filial throng
    This mother-head adores.

This bringer of world-wealth, whereof
    None may compute the worth,
Is possibly of no account
    To anyone on earth.

Her cap and spectacles, that mean
    Dim eyes and scanty hairs,
The humble symbols of her state –
    The only crown she wears.

Lacking a kingdom and a court,
    A relic of the past,
Almost a cumberer of the ground –
    That is our queen at last.

But still not wholly without place,
    Nor quite bereft of power;
A useful stopgap – a resource
    In many a troubled hour.

She darns the stockings, keeps the house,
    The nurseless infant tends,
While the young matrons and the men
    Pursue their various ends –

Too keen-set on their great affairs,
    Or little plays and pranks,
The things and people of their world,
    To give her thought or thanks –

The children on whom all her thought
    And time and love were spent
Through half a century of years!
    Yet is she well content.

The schooling of those fiery years,
    It has not been for nought;
A large philosophy of life
    Has self-less service taught.

The outlook from the heights attained
    By climbings sore and slow
Discovers worlds of wisdom, hid
    From clearest eyes below.

Watching their joyous setting forth
    To mingle with their kind,
With scarce a pang, with ne'er a grudge,
    At being left behind.

them be young, as I was young,
And happy while they may'…
og that waits the night in peace
since it has had its day.

Cambridge (1844–1926)

Granny Grey Pow

Auld Granny Grey Pow,
    Fetch the bairnies in;
Bring them frae the Scaur Heid,
    Where they mak' sic din.
Chase them frae the washin' pool,
    Thrang at skippin' stanes –
Auld Granny Grey Pow,
    Gather hame the weans.

Bring in Rab to get him wash'd,
    Weel I ken the loon
Canna dae unless he be
    Dirt frae fit to croon.
Tam and Wull are just the same,
    For a' I tak' sic pains –
Auld Granny Grey Pow,
    Gather hame the weans.

Fetch my ain wee Jeanie in,
    Mammy's pet o' a';
Jamie, wha aye slips aboot,
    And speaks nae much ava.
Bring them to their cosie bed,
    There to rest their banes –
Auld Granny Grey Pow,
    Gather hame the weans.

Here they come; ill Rab is first
  Tam an' Wull ahin';
Jamie has wee Jeanie's han',
  An' baith begin to rin.
Whaten faces hae they a'
  Dirt laid on in grains!
Auld Granny Grey Pow,
  Gather hame the weans.

In they toddle, ane by ane;
  Wull, wha's aye the fule,
Quarrels wi' ill Rab aboot
  Whase nicht it's for the stule.
Jeanie hunkers at my feet,
  While sleep upon her gains –
Auld Granny Grey Pow,
  I hae a' my weans.

Auld Granny Grey Pow,
  Steek the door fu' ticht,
No a wean, if I can help,
  Gangs ower the door this nicht.
There they lie in cosie beds,
  The morn's wark in their brains –
Auld Granny Grey Pow,
  Bless my sleepin' weans.

Mony a fit we hae to gang,
  Mony a care to deave;
Joy an' woe are thread aboot
  In the wab we weave.

Let us work it to the en',
   So that He who reigns
May whisper, when life's gloamin' comes,
   'Gather hame the weans.'

Alexander Anderson 1845–1909

Grandma's Prayer

I pray that, risen from the dead,
    I may in glory stand –
A crown, perhaps, upon my head,
    But a needle in my hand.

I've never learned to sing or play,
    So let no harp be mine;
From birth unto my dying day,
    Plain sewing's been my line.

Therefore, accustomed to the end
    To plying useful stitches,
I'll be content if asked to mend
    The little angels' breeches.

Eugene Field (1850–95)

The Happy Household

It's when the birds go piping and the daylight slowly breaks,
That, clamoring for his dinner, our precious baby wakes;
Then it's sleep no more for baby, and it's sleep no more
    for me,
For, when he wants his dinner, why it's dinner it must be!
And of that lacteal fluid he partakes with great ado,
    While gran'ma laughs,
    And gran'pa laughs,
    And wife, she laughs,
    And I – well, I laugh, too!

You'd think, to see us carrying on about that little tad,
That, like as not, that baby was the first we'd ever had;
But, sakes alive! He isn't, yet we people make a fuss
As if the only baby in the world had come to us!
And, morning, noon, and night-time, whatever he may do,
    Gran'ma, she laughs,
    Gran'pa, he laughs,
    Wife, she laughs,
    And I, of course, laugh, too!

But once – a likely spell ago – when that poor little chick
From teething or from some such ill of infancy fell sick,
You wouldn't know us people as the same that went about
A-feelin' good all over, just to hear him crow and shout;
And, though the doctor poohed our fears and said he'd
    pull him through,
    Old gran'ma cried,
    And gran'pa cried,
    And wife, she cried,
    And I – yes, I cried, too!

It makes us all feel good to have a baby on the place,
With his everlastin' crowing and his dimpling, dumpling face;
The patter of his pinky feet makes music everywhere,
And when he shakes those fists of his, good-bye to every care!
No matter what our trouble is, when he begins to coo,
    Old gran'ma laughs,
    And gran'pa laughs,
    Wife, she laughs,
    And I – you bet, I laugh, too!

Eugene Field (1850–95)

The Cunnin' Little Thing

When baby wakes of mornings,
Then it's wake, ye people all!
For another day
Of song and play
Has come at our darling's call!
And, till she gets her dinner,
She makes the welkin ring,
And she won't keep still till she's had her fill –
The cunnin' little thing!

When baby goes a-walking,
Oh, how her paddies fly!
For that's the way
The babies say
To other folk 'by-by';
The trees bend down to kiss her,
And the birds in rapture sing,
As there she stands and waves her hands –
The cunnin' little thing!

When baby goes a-rocking
In her bed at close of day,
At hide-and-seek
On her dainty cheek
The dreams and the dimples play;
Then it's sleep in the tender kisses
The guardian angels bring
From the Far Above to my sweetest love –
You cunnin' little thing!

Eugene Field (1850–95)

In Grandmamma's Kitchen

In grandmamma's kitchen, things got in a riot –
The cream in a pot on the shelf,
Where everything always seemed peaceful and quiet,
Got whipped, for I heard it myself.
And grandmamma said – such a queer thing to say,
That it made some things better to whip them that way.

Some bold naughty eggs that refused to be eaten,
On toast with their brothers may be,
Were stripped of their clothing and cruelly beaten
Right where all the dishes could see.
And grandmamma said though the poor things might ache,
The harder the beating, the lighter the cake.

The bright golden butter was petted and patted
And coaxed to be shapely and good.
But it finally had to be taken and spatted
Right hard with a paddle of wood.
When grandmamma carried the round balls away,
The buttermilk sulked, and looked sour all day.

The water declared that the coffee was muddy,
But an egg settled that little fuss.
Then the steak and the gridiron got in a bloody
And terrible broil! Such a muss!
And a flat-iron spat at grandma in the face,
And I ran away from the quarrelsome place.

Ella Wheeler Wilcox (1850–1919)

Extract from Black Bonnets

A day of seeming innocence,
A glorious sun and sky,
And, just above my picket fence,
Black Bonnet passing by.
In knitted gloves and quaint old dress,
Without a spot or smirch,
Her worn face lit with peacefulness,
Old Granny goes to church.

Her hair is richly white, like milk,
That long ago was fair –
And glossy still the old black silk
She keeps for 'chapel wear';
Her bonnet, of a bygone style,
That long has passed away,
She must have kept a weary while
Just as it is to-day.

The parasol of days gone by –
Old days that seemed the best –
The hymn and prayer books carried high
Against her warm, thin breast;
As she had clasped – come smiles come tears,
Come hardship, aye, and worse –
On market days, through faded years,
The slender household purse.

Although the road is rough and steep,
She takes it with a will,
For, since she hushed her first to sleep
Her way has been uphill.
Instinctively I bare my head
(A sinful one, alas!)
Whene'er I see, by church bells led,
Brave Old Black Bonnet pass.

For she has known the cold and heat
And dangers of the Track:
Has fought bush-fires to save the wheat
And little home Out Back.
By barren creeks the Bushman loves,
By stockyard, hut, and pen,
The withered hands in those old gloves
Have done the work of men.

They called it 'Service' long ago
When Granny yet was young,
And in the chapel, sweet and low,
As girls her daughters sung.
And when in church she bends her head
(But not as others do)
She sees her loved ones, and her dead
And hears their voices too.

Fair as the Saxons in her youth,
Not forward, and not shy;
And strong in healthy life and truth
As after years went by:
She often laughed with sinners vain,
Yet passed from faith to sight –
God gave her beauty back again
The more her hair grew white.

By verdant swath and ivied wall
The congregation's seen –
White nothings where the shadows fall,
Black blots against the green.
The dull, suburban people meet
And buzz in little groups,
While down the white steps to the street
A quaint old figure stoops.

And then along my picket fence
Where staring wallflowers grow –
World-wise Old Age, and Common-sense!
Black Bonnet, nodding slow.
But not alone; for on each side
A little dot attends
In snowy frock and sash of pride,
And these are Granny's friends.

To them her mind is clear and bright,
Her old ideas are new;
They know her 'real talk' is right,
Her 'fairy talk' is true.
And they converse as grown-ups may,
When all the news is told;
The one so wisely young to-day,
The two so wisely old.

At home, with dinner waiting there,
She smooths her hair and face,
And puts her bonnet by with care
And dons a cap of lace.
The table minds its p's and q's
Lest one perchance be hit
By some rare dart which is a part
Of her old-fashioned wit.

Her son and son's wife are asleep,
She puts her apron on –
The quiet house is hers to keep,
With all the youngsters gone.
There's scarce a sound of dish on dish
Or cup slipped into cup,
When left alone, as is her wish,
Black Bonnet 'washes up.'

Henry Lawson (1867–1922)

Grandma's Recipes

This has always puzzled me, just how much is a pinch?
These recipes of dear Grandma's surely are no cinch.
A 'snip' of this, a 'dab' of that, a 'lump' of something else,
Then 'beat it for a little while', or, 'stir until it melts.'
I have to be a wizard to decipher what she meant,
By all these strange proportions in her cookbook worn and bent.
How much nutmeg in the doughnuts? Grandma wouldn't flinch,
As she said, with twinkling eyes, 'Oh, just about a pinch.'
There must have been in her wise head a measuring device,
That told her just how much to use of sugar, salt and spice.

Author Unknown

FUN & GAMES

The Baby's Dance

Dance little baby, dance up high,
Never mind baby, mother is by;
Crow and caper, caper and crow,
There little baby, there you go;
Up to the ceiling, down to the ground,
Backwards and forwards, round and round;
Dance little baby, and mother shall sing,
With the merry coral, ding, ding, ding.

Ann Taylor (1782–1866)

Extract from Old Memories

Bright flashes of sunshine, sweet snatches of song,
Warm gushings of kindness, come thrilling along
The chords of old memories, melting the tone,
And sweet the weird voices of years that are gone.

I hear the brisk hum of the dear spinning wheel;
Again, the kind hand of Old Granny I feel,
As she strokes down my hair, singing soft, as I stood
By her side, the 'Blaeberries' or 'Babes of the Wood.'

Janet Hamilton (1795–1873)

Grandmamma and the Fairies

In the pattern of the curtains
Upon Grandmamma's bed,
You may see the parks where fairies
Their nightly measures tread.
The white parts are their gravel walks,
Where freely they advance;
The green parts are the careful lawns,
Where they may only dance.
All the walks go winding,
And twisting in and out,
Where the little cheerful creatures
Wander and play about.
And two or three, more bold than wise,
Behind the pillow peep,
And whisper to their waiting friends
That Grandmamma's asleep.
Then they begin to rustle
Among the falling folds;
And some of them are singing,
And some have coughs and colds;
And some have little castanets,
And some have little drums;
And some (who fly) will stop and perch
On Grandmamma's thumbs.
Grandmamma grows restless,
And turns upon the bed;
She thinks she has been waken'd
By noises in her head.
And many a little threat of cramp

Across her frame she feels;
And many a small rheumatic pinch
About her hands and heels.
Grandmamma grows plaintive:
When she was young, she says,
The long soft nights of slumber
Were pleasant as the days;
The steepest mountain in the world
Seem'd but a sunny slope;
And if the fairies talked at all,
They only talk'd of hope.
She'll tell us all at breakfast
She had a wretched night;
The furniture was creaking,
The pillows were not right.
With bolted door and windows wedged,
The care was all in vain;
For there were noises in her room
Which nothing can explain.
Then all suggest a reason:
Miss Grey alludes to gnats,
Aunt Hetty talks of robbers,
And Uncle James of rats.
Papa says, 'Girls will brush their hair,
Such chattering little folks!'
Mamma says, 'George was sitting up:
You know how hard he smokes!'
But no one seems to notice,
While thus they fuss and guess,
A little whiff of laughter
Among the water-cress.

A fairy spy is station'd there,
Commission'd to record,
In a very short-hand summary,
Each blundering human word.
If Grandmamma is clever,
When next the curtains shake,
She'll take her chance of fairies,
And tell them she's awake.
She'll let them see she knows their tricks,
And that they're far too late
To take a fine old lady in,
Who's turn'd of seventy-eight.
A little show of spirit
Would bring them to their knees,
Would make them full of service,
Where now they only tease.
And then they might bring back again
That sweet time pass'd away,
When every night was full of sleep,
Of pleasure every day.
That village shop, they'll show her,
Under the chestnut shade,
With the glorious sugar-candy,
Which is no longer made;
With the sheets of fine stage-characters,
And the scissors with no points,
And those delightful wooden dolls,
With pegs in all their joints:
That field with lofty hedges;
That elm-tree with a crest,
Where a blackbird sat so often,

She knows it had a nest;
And where she found the primroses
So early in the year;
And where she thinks she saw a snake
When nobody was near:
That garden with the peaches
Train'd on the old red wall;
The scent of that first myrtle
She pluck'd for her first ball;
And where she found a bouquet once,
Such fragrance and such tints!
I think it came from Grandpapa:
But that she never hints.
She'll tell us all at breakfast
She had a lovely night;
And Grandpapa will whisper,
Because she looks so bright,
'You'll never match those eyes, my dears'
(He said this once, you know);
'They're even finer than they were,
Ah, sixty years ago.'

Menella Bute Smedley (1820–77)

Yet Gentle Will the Griffin Be
(What Grandpa told the Children)

The moon? It is a griffin's egg,
Hatching to-morrow night.
And how the little boys will watch
With shouting and delight
To see him break the shell and stretch
And creep across the sky.
The boys will laugh. The little girls,
I fear, may hide and cry.
Yet gentle will the griffin be,
Most decorous and fat,
And walk up to the milky way
And lap it like a cat.

Vachel Lindsay (1879–1931)

Grandmother's Spring

'In my young days,' the grandmother said (Nodding her head,
Where cap and curls were as white as snow),
'In my young days, when we used to go
Rambling,
Scrambling;
Each little dirty hand in hand,
Like a chain of daisies, a comical band
Of neighbours' children, seriously straying,
Really and truly going a-Maying,
My mother would bid us linger,
And lifting a slender, straight forefinger,

Would say –
"Little Kings and Queens of the May,
Listen to me!
If you want to be
Every one of you very good
In that beautiful, beautiful, beautiful wood,
Where the little birds' heads get so turned with delight,
That some of them sing all night:
Whatever you pluck,
Leave some for good luck;
Picked from the stalk, or pulled up by the root,
From overhead, or from underfoot,
Water-wonders of pond or brook;
Wherever you look,
And whatever you find –
Leave something behind:
Some for the Naïads,
Some for the Dryads,
And a bit for the Nixies, and the Pixies.'"

'After all these years,' the grandame said,
Lifting her head,
'I think I can hear my mother's voice
Above all other noise,
Saying, "Hearken, my child!
There is nothing more destructive and wild,
No wild bull with his horns,
No wild-briar with clutching thorns,
No pig that routs in your garden-bed,
No robber with ruthless tread,
More reckless and rude,

And wasteful of all things lovely and good,
Than a child, with the face of a boy and the ways of a bear,
Who doesn't care;
Or some little ignorant minx
Who never thinks.
Now I never knew so stupid an elf,
That he couldn't think and care for himself.
Oh, little sisters and little brothers,
Think for others, and care for others!
And of all that your little fingers find,
Leave something behind,
For love of those that come after:
Some, perchance, to cool tired eyes in the moss that stifled
     your laughter!
Pluck, children, pluck!
But leave, for good luck,
Some for the Naïads,
And some for the Dryads,
And a bit for the Nixies, and the Pixies!'"

'We were very young,' the grandmother said,
Smiling and shaking her head;
'And when one is young,
One listens with half an ear, and speaks with a hasty tongue;
So with shouted Yeses,
And promises sealed with kisses,
Hand-in-hand we started again,
A chubby chain,
Stretching the whole wide width of the lane;
Or in broken links of twos and threes,
For greater ease

Of rambling,
And scrambling,
By the stile and the road,
That goes to the beautiful, beautiful wood;
By the brink of the gloomy pond,
To the top of the sunny hill beyond,
By hedge and by ditch, by marsh and by mead,
By little byways that lead
To mysterious bowers;
Or to spots where, for those who know,
There grow,
In certain out-o'-way nooks, rare ferns and uncommon flowers.
There were flowers everywhere,
Censing the summer air,
Till the giddy bees went rolling home
To their honeycomb,
And when we smelt at our posies,
The little fairies inside the flowers rubbed coloured dust on
    our noses,
Or pricked us till we cried aloud for snuffing the dear dog-roses.
But above all our noise,
I kept thinking I heard my mother's voice.
But it may have been only a fairy joke,
For she was at home, and I sometimes thought it was really
    the flowers that spoke.
From the Foxglove in its pride,
To the Shepherd's Purse by the bare road-side;
From the snap-jack heart of the Starwort frail,
To meadows full of Milkmaids pale,
And Cowslips loved by the nightingale.
Rosette of the tasselled Hazel-switch,

Sky-blue star of the ditch;
Dandelions like mid-day suns;
Bindweed that runs;
Butter and Eggs with the gaping lips,
Sweet Hawthorn that hardens to haws, and Roses
    that die into hips;
Lords-with-their-Ladies cheek-by-jowl,
In purple surcoat and pale-green cowl;
Family groups of Primroses fair;
Orchids rare;
Velvet Bee-orchis that never can sting,
Butterfly-orchis which never takes wing,
Robert-the-Herb with strange sweet scent,
And crimson leaf when summer is spent:
Clustering neighbourly,
All this gay company,
Said to us seemingly –
"Pluck, children, pluck!
But leave some for good luck:
Some for the Naïads,
Some for the Dryads,
And a bit for the Nixies, and the Pixies,"'

'I was but a maid,' the grandame said,
'When my mother was dead;
And many a time have I stood.
In that beautiful wood,
To dream that through every woodland noise,
Through the cracking
Of twigs and the bending of bracken,
Through the rustling

Of leaves in the breeze,
And the bustling
Of dark-eyed, tawny-tailed squirrels flitting about the trees,
Through the purling and trickling cool
Of the streamlet that feeds the pool,
I could hear her voice.
Should I wonder to hear it? Why?
Are the voices of tender wisdom apt to die?
And now, though I'm very old,
And the air, that used to feel fresh, strikes chilly and cold,
On a sunny day when I potter
About the garden, or totter
To the seat from whence I can see, below,
The marsh and the meadows I used to know,
Bright with the bloom of the flowers that blossomed there
    long ago;
Then, as if it were yesterday,
I fancy I hear them say –
'Pluck, children, pluck,
But leave some for good luck;
Picked from the stalk, or pulled up by the root,
From overhead, or from underfoot,
Water-wonders of pond or brook;
Wherever you look,
And whatever your little fingers find,
Leave something behind:
Some for the Naïads,
And some for the Dryads,
And a bit for the Nixies, and the Pixies.'

Juliana Horatia Ewing (1841–85)

Granny

Granny's come to our house,
    And ho! My lawzy-daisy!
All the childern round the place
    Is ist a-runnin' crazy!
Fetched a cake fer little Jake,
    And fetched a pie fer Nanny,
And fetched a pear fer all the pack
    That runs to kiss their Granny!

Lucy Ellen's in her lap,
    And Wade and Silas Walker
Both's a-ridin' on her foot,
    And 'Pollos on the rocker;
And Marthy's twins, from Aunt Marinn's,
    And little Orphant Annie,
All's a-eatin' gingerbread
    And giggle-un at Granny!

Tells us all the fairy tales
    Ever thought er wundered,
And 'bundance o' other stories –
    Bet she knows a hunderd!
Bob's the one fer 'Whittington,'
    And 'Golden Locks' fer Fanny!
Hear 'em laugh and clap their hands,
    Listenin' at Granny!

'Jack the Giant-Killer' 's good;
    And 'Bean-Stalk"s another!
So's the one of 'Cinderell"
    And her old godmother;
That-un's best of all the rest,
    Bestest one of any,
Where the mices scampers home
    Like we runs to Granny!

Granny's come to our house,
    Ho! My lawzy-daisy!
All the childern round the place
    Is ist a-runnin' crazy!
Fetched a cake fer little Jake,
    And fetched a pie fer Nanny,
And fetched a pear fer all the pack
    That runs to kiss their Granny!

James Whitcomb Riley (1849–1916)

Jack-in-the-Box
(Grandfather, musing)

In childish days! O memory,
You bring such curious things to me!
Laughs to the lip, tears to the eye,
In looking on the gifts that lie
Like broken playthings scattered o'er
Imagination's nursery floor!

Did these old hands once click the key
That let 'Jack's' box-lid upward fly,
And that blear-eyed, fur-whiskered elf
Leap, as though frightened at himself,
And quiveringly lean and stare
At me, his jailer, laughing there?

A child then! Now, I only know
They call me very old; and so
They will not let me have my way,
But uselessly I sit all day
Here by the chimney-jamb, and poke
The lazy fire, and smoke and smoke,
And watch the wreaths swoop up the flue,
And chuckle, ay, I often do,
Seeing again, all vividly,
Jack-in-the-box leap, as in glee
To see how much he looks like me!

... They talk. I can't hear what they say –
But I am glad, clean through and through
Sometimes, in fancying that they
Are saying, 'Sweet, that fancy strays
In age back to our childish days!'

James Whitcomb Riley (1849–1916)

Five Little Toes in the Morning

This little toe is hungry,
This little toe is too,
This toe lies abed like a sleepy head,
And this toe cries 'Boo-hoo.'
This toe big and tall is the smartest of all
For he pops into stocking and shoe.

Ella Wheeler Wilcox (1850–1919)

Five Little Toes at Night

This little toe is tired,
This little toe needs rocking,
This little toe is sleepy you know,
But this little toe keeps talking,
This toe big and tall is the mischief of all,
For he made a great hole in his stocking.

Ella Wheeler Wilcox (1850–1919)

'One, Two, Three'

It was an old, old, old, old lady,
And a boy that was half-past three;
And the way that they played together
Was beautiful to see.

She couldn't go running or jumping,
And the boy, no more could he;
For he was a thin litte fellow,
With a thin little twisted knee.

They sat in the yellow sunlight,
Out under the maple tree;
And the game that they played I'll tell you,
Just as it was told to me.

It was Hide-and-Go-Seek they were playing,
Though you've never have known it to be –
With an old, old, old, old lady,
And a boy with a twisted knee.

The boy would bend his face down
On his one little sound right knee,
And he'd guess where she was hiding,
In guesses One, Two, Three!

'You are in the china-closet!'
He would cry, and laugh with glee –
It wasn't the china closet,
But he still had Two and Three.

'You are up in papa's big bedroom,
In the chest with the queer old key!'
And she said: 'You are warm and warmer;
But you're not quite right,' said she.

'It can't be the little cupboard
Where mamma's things used to be –
So it must be the clothes-press, Gran'ma!'
And he found her with his Three.

Then she covered her face with her fingers,
That were wrinkled and white and wee,
And she guessed where the boy was hiding,
With a One and a Two and a Three.

And they never had stirred from their places,
Right under the maple tree –
This old, old, old, old lady
And the boy with the lame little knee –
This dear, dear, dear old lady,
And the boy who was half-past three.

Henry Cuyler Bunner (1855–96)

The Banana's Lullaby

When grandma wished to keep her fruit
    Her apples she would take
And put them on a bed of straw
    At rest, but wide awake;
But newer days have newer modes,
    And now, that it may keep,
They give an orange opiates
    And sing it off to sleep.

And they're telling bedtime stories to bananas,
    And rocking little raspberries to rest.
They will dope an apple silly,
And it wakes in Piccadilly
    From a beauty sleep that makes it look its best.

It seems a heartless kind of trick
    To play on helpless pears;
To lull them off to slumberland
    And soothe their nervous cares,
Only to wake them up again,
    Weeks after, on a plate,
On the day of execution
    To announce their cruel fate.

But they're telling bedtime stories to bananas,
    And putting plums to by-by on a ship,
And they never have a notion
They have been across the ocean,
    So they even miss the pleasure of the trip.

C.J. Dennis (1876–1958)

Grandfather's Love

They said he sent his love to me,
They wouldn't put it in my hand,
And when I asked them where it was
They said I couldn't understand.

I thought they must have hidden it,
I hunted for it all the day,
And when I told them so at night
They smiled and turned their heads away.

They say that love is something kind,
That I can never see or touch.
I wish he'd sent me something else,
I like his cough-drops twice as much.

Sara Teasdale (1884–1933)

Butterfly Laughter

In the middle of our porridge plates
There was a blue butterfly painted
And each morning we tried who should reach the
butterfly first.
Then the Grandmother said: 'Do not eat the poor
butterfly.'
That made us laugh.
Always she said it and always it started us laughing.
It seemed such a sweet little joke.
I was certain that one fine morning
The butterfly would fly out of our plates,
Laughing the teeniest laugh in the world,
And perch on the Grandmother's lap.

Katherine Mansfield (1888–1923)

The Candle

By my bed, on a little round table
The Grandmother placed a candle.
She gave me three kisses telling me they were three dreams
And tucked me in just where I loved being tucked.
Then she went out of the room and the door was shut.
I lay still, waiting for my three dreams to talk;
But they were silent.
Suddenly I remember giving her three kisses back.
Perhaps, by mistake, I had given my three little dreams
I sat up in bed.
The room grew big, oh, bigger far than a church.
The wardrobe, quite by itself, as big as a house.
And the jug on the washstand smiled at me:
It was not a friendly smile.
I looked at the basket-chair where my clothes lay folded:
The chair gave a creak as though it were listening for something.
Perhaps it was coming alive and going to dress in my clothes.
But the awful thing was the window:
I could not think what was outside.
No tree to be seen, I was sure,
No nice little plant or friendly pebbly path.
Why did she pull the blind down every night?
It was better to know.
I crunched my teeth and crept out of bed,
I peeped through a slit of the blind.
There was nothing at all to be seen.
But hundreds of friendly candles all over the sky

In remembrance of frightened children.
I went back to bed…
The three dreams started singing a little song.

Katherine Mansfield (1888–1923)

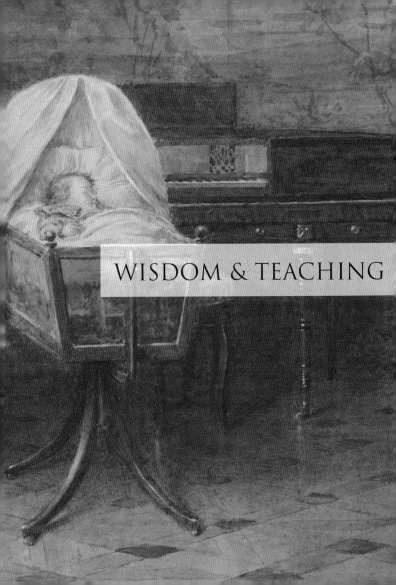

WISDOM & TEACHING

My Grandmother Said

My Grandmother said, 'Now isn't it queer,
That boys must whistle and girls must sing?
But that's how 'tis!' – I heard her say –
'The same tomorrow as yesterday.'

Author Unknown

Extract from The Sermon in the Stocking

The supper is over, the hearth is swept,
And in the wood-fire's glow
The children cluster to hear a tale
Of that time so long ago,

When grandmamma's hair was golden brown,
And the warm blood came and went
O'er the face that could scarce have been sweeter then
Than now in its rich content.

The face is wrinkled and careworn now,
And the golden hair is gray;
But the light that shone in the young girl's eyes
Has never gone away.

And her needles catch the fire's light
As in and out they go,
With the clicking music that grandma loves
Shaping the stocking's toe.

And the waking children love it too,
For they know the stocking song
Brings many a tale to grandma's mind
Which they shall hear ere long.

But it brings no story of olden time
To grandma's heart tonight,
Only a ditty quaint and short
Is sung by the needles bright.

'Life is a stocking,' grandma says,
'And yours is just begun;
But I am knitting the toe of mine,
And my work is almost done.

'With merry hearts we begin to knit,
And the ribbing is almost play;
Some are gay-coloured, and some are white,
And some are ashen gray.

'But most are made of many a hue,
With many a stitch set wrong,
And many a row to be sadly ripped
Ere the whole is fair and strong.

'There are long plain stretches without a break,
That in youth are hard to bear;
And many a weary tear is dropped
As we fashion the heel with care.

'But the saddest, happiest time is that
We court and yet would shun,
When our Heavenly Father breaks the thread,
And says our work is done.'

Author Unknown

Cleanliness

Come, my little Robert, near –
Fie! What filthy hands are here?
Who that e'er could understand
The rare structure of a hand,
With its branching fingers fine,
Work itself of hands divine,
Strong, yet delicately knit,
For ten thousand uses fit,
Overlaid with so clear skin
You may see the blood within,
And the curious palm, disposed
In such lines, some have supposed
You may read the fortunes there
By the figures that appear,
Who this hand would choose to cover
With a crust of dirt all over,
Till it looked in hue and shape
Like the fore-foot of an ape?
Man or boy that works or plays
In the fields or the highways,
May, without offence or hurt,
From the soil contract a dirt,
Which the next clear spring or river
Washes out and out for ever –
But to cherish stains impure,
Soil deliberate to endure,
On the skin to fix a stain
Till it works into the grain,

Argues a degenerate mind,
Sordid, slothful, ill inclined,
Wanting in that self-respect
Which does virtue best protect.

All-endearing cleanliness,
Virtue next to godliness,
Easiest, cheapest, needfull'st duty,
To the body health and beauty,
Who that's human would refuse it,
When a little water does it?

Charles Lamb (1775–1834)

For My Grandsons, Eddy and Ally

I here engage
Upon this page
   A picture to portray,
Of two of an age
Yet neither a sage,
   But right honest hearts have they.
Each loves to play
And have his own way,
Yet I'm happy to say
   They quarrel, if ever, but seldom.
Though competent quite
To maintain their own right,
And even to fight,
   Yet peace to their bosom is welcome.
Both go to school,
And learn by rule
   That in neither a dunce we may find;
Both read and spell
And like it well;
   Thus with pleasure is profit combined.
One's eyes are black,
The other's blue;
   They both have honest hearts and true,
   And love each other dearly:
One's father, is brother

To the other one's mother,
    So cousins german are they most clearly;
Each has a father,
And each has a mother,
    And both do dearly love him;
But neither a sister,
And neither a brother,
    To play with, or to plague him.
And here I propose,
Ere I come to a close,
    A little advice to give;
To which if they heed,
They'll be better indeed,
    And happier as long as they live.
Be sure to mind
Your parents kind,
    And do nothing to vex or tease them;
But through each day
Heed what they say,
    And strive to obey and please them.
Take not in vain
God's holy name,
Do not work,
Do not play
On God's holy day,
    Nor from church stay away;
Always bear it in mind
To be gentle and kind,
And friends you will find,
And hearts to you bind,

I am sure I may venture to say.
And when you're men,
Who sees you then
    I hope in you models will see,
Of good and great,
In Church and State,
    Whose lips with your lives agree.

Mary Ann H.T. Bigelow (∂. 1870)

About the Little Girl that Beat Her Sister

Go, go, my naughty girl, and kiss
    Your little sister dear;
I must not have such things as this,
    And noisy quarrels here.

What! Little children scratch and fight,
    That ought to be so mild;
Oh! Mary, it's a shocking sight
    To see an angry child.

I can't imagine, for my part,
    The reason for your folly;
She did not do you any hurt
    By playing with your dolly.

See, see, the little tears that run
    Fast from her watery eye:
Come, my sweet innocent, have done,
    'Twill do no good to cry.

Go, Mary, wipe her tears away,
    And make it up with kisses:
And never turn a pretty play
    To such a pet as this is.

Ann Taylor (1782–1866)

Meddlesome Matty

One ugly trick has often spoil'd
    The sweetest and the best;
Matilda, though a pleasant child,
    One ugly trick possess'd,
Which, like a cloud before the skies,
Hid all her better qualities.

Sometimes she'd lift the tea-pot lid,
    To peep at what was in it,
Or tilt the kettle, if you did
    But turn your back a minute.
In vain you told her not to touch,
Her trick of meddling grew so much.

Her grandmamma went out one day,
    And by mistake she laid
Her spectacles and snuff-box gay
    Too near the little maid;
'Ah! Well,' thought she, 'I'll try them on,
As soon as grandmamma is gone.'

Forthwith she placed upon her nose
    The glasses large and wide;
And looking round, as I suppose,
    The snuff-box too she spied:
'Oh! What a pretty box is that;
I'll open it,' said little Matt.

'I know that grandmamma would say,
  "Don't meddle with it, dear;"
But then, she's far enough away,
  And no one else is near:
Besides, what can there be amiss
In opening such a box as this?'

So thumb and finger went to work
　　To move the stubborn lid,
And presently a mighty jerk
　　The mighty mischief did;
For all at once, ah! Woeful case,
The snuff came puffing in her face.

Poor eyes, and nose, and mouth, beside
　　A dismal sight presented;
In vain, as bitterly she cried,
　　Her folly she repented.
In vain she ran about for ease;
She could do nothing now but sneeze.

She dash'd the spectacles away,
　　To wipe her tingling eyes,
And as in twenty bits they lay,
　　Her grandmamma she spies.
'Heyday! And what's the matter now?'
Says grandmamma, with lifted brow.

Matilda, smarting with the pain,
　　And tingling still, and sore,
Made many a promise to refrain
　　From meddling evermore.
And 'tis a fact, as I have heard,
She ever since has kept her word.

Ann Taylor (1782–1866)

The Power of Words

'Tis a strange mystery, the power of words!
Life is in them, and death. A word can send
The crimson colour hurrying to the cheek.
Hurrying with many meanings; or can turn
The current cold and deadly to the heart.
Anger and fear are in them; grief and joy
Are on their sound; yet slight, impalpable:
A word is but a breath of passing air.

Letitia Elizabeth Landon (1802–38)

Take the World as it Is

Take the world as it is! There are good and bad in it,
　　And good and bad will be from now to the end;
And they, who expect to make saints in a minute,
　　Are in danger of marring more hearts than they'll mend.
If ye wish to be happy ne'er seek for the faults,
　　Or you're sure to find something or other amiss;
'Mid much that debases, and much that exalts,
　　The world's not a bad one if left as it is.

Take the world as it is! If the surface be shining,
　　Ne'er rake up the sediment hidden below!
There's wisdom in this, but there's none in repining
　　O'er things which can rarely be mended, we know.
There's beauty around us, which let us enjoy;
　　And chide not, unless it may be with a kiss;
Though Earth's not the Heaven we thought when a boy,
　　There's something to live for, if ta'en as it is.

Take the world as it is! With its smiles and its sorrow,
　　Its love and its friendship, its falsehood and truth,
Its schemes that depend on the breath of to-morrow,
　　Its hopes which pass by like the dreams of our youth:
Yet, oh! Whilst the light of affection may shine,
　　The heart in itself hath a fountain of bliss;
In the worst there's some spark of a nature divine,
　　And the wisest and best take the world as it is.

Charles Swain (1803–74)

Extract from **What We All Think**

That age was older once than now,
In spite of locks untimely shed,
Or silvered on the youthful brow;
That babes make love and children wed.

That sunshine had a heavenly glow,
Which faded with those 'good old days'
When winters came with deeper snow,
And autumns with a softer haze.

That – mother, sister, wife, or child –
The 'best of women' each has known.
Were school-boys ever half so wild?
How young the grandpapas have grown!

That but for this our souls were free,
And but for that our lives were blest;
That in some season yet to be
Our cares will leave us time to rest.

Whene'er we groan with ache or pain –
Some common ailment of the race –
Though doctors think the matter plain –
That ours is 'a peculiar case.'

Oliver Wendell Holmes Snr (1809–94)

A Word of Wisdom

Make the best of all things,
　　As thy lot is cast?
Whatsoe'er we call things
　　All is well at last,
If meanwhile, in cheerful power,
Patience rules the suffering hour.

Make the best of all things,
　　Howsoe'er they be;
Change may well befall things
　　If it's ill with thee;
And if well, this present joy
Let no future fears destroy.

Make the best of all things,
　　That is Wisdom's word;
In the day of small things
　　Is its comfort heard,
And its blessing soothes not less
Any heyday of success.

Make the best of all things;
　　Discontent's old leaven
Falsely would forestall things
　　Antedating heaven,
But smile thou and rest content,
Bearing trials wisely sent.

Martin Farqubar Tupper (1810–89)

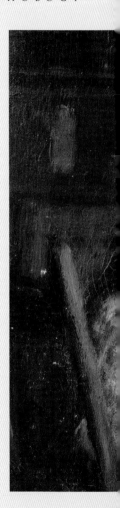

Extract from Somebody's Mother

The woman was old and ragged and gray
And bent with the chill of the Winter's day.

The street was wet with a recent snow
And the woman's feet were aged and slow.

Down the street, with laughter and shout,
Glad in the freedom of 'school let out,'

Came the boys like a flock of sheep,
Hailing the snow piled white and deep.

Past the woman so old and gray
Hastened the children on their way.

Nor offered a helping hand to her –
So meek, so timid, afraid to stir

Lest the carriage wheels or the horses' feet
Should crowd her down in the slippery street.

At last came one of the merry troop,
The gayest laddie of all the group:

He paused beside her and whispered low,
'I'll help you cross, if you wish to go.'

Her aged hand on his strong young arm
She placed, and so, without hurt or harm,

He guided the trembling feet along,
Proud that his own were firm and strong.

Then back again to his friends he went,
His young heart happy and well content.

'She's somebody's mother, boys, you know,
For all she's aged and poor and slow.

'And I hope some fellow will lend a hand
To help my mother, you understand,

'If ever she's poor and old and gray,
When her own dear boy is far away.'

And 'somebody's mother' bowed low her head
In her home that night, and the prayer she said

Was 'God be kind to the noble boy,
Who is somebody's son, and pride and joy!'

Mabel Down Northam Brine (1816–1913)

The Hand that Rocks the Cradle

Blessings on the hand of women!
Angels guard its strength and grace,
In the palace, cottage, hovel,
Oh, no matter where the place;
Would that never storms assailed it,
Rainbows ever gently curled;
For the hand that rocks the cradle
Is the hand that rules the world.

Infancy's the tender fountain,
Power may with beauty flow,
Mother's first to guide the streamlets,
From them souls unresting grow –
Grow on for the good or evil,
Sunshine streamed or evil hurled;
For the hand that rocks the cradle
Is the hand that rules the world.

Woman, how divine your mission
Here upon our natal sod!
Keep, oh, keep the young heart open
Always to the breath of God!
All true trophies of the ages
Are from mother-love impearled;
For the hand that rocks the cradle
Is the hand that rules the world.

Blessings on the hand of women!
Fathers, sons, and daughters cry,
And the sacred song is mingled
With the worship in the sky –
Mingles where no tempest darkens,
Rainbows evermore are hurled;
For the hand that rocks the cradle
Is the hand that rules the world.

William Ross Wallace (1819–81)

The Willow-Man

There once was a Willow, and he was very old,
And all his leaves fell off from him, and left him in the cold;
But ere the rude winter could buffet him with snow,
There grew upon his hoary head a crop of Mistletoe.

All wrinkled and furrowed was this old Willow's skin,
His taper fingers trembled, and his arms were very thin;
Two round eyes and hollow, that stared but did not see,
And sprawling feet that never walked, had this most
    ancient tree.

A Dame who dwelt near was the only one who knew
That every year upon his head the Christmas berries grew;
And when the Dame cut them, she said – it was her whim –
'A merry Christmas to you, Sir!' and left a bit for him.

'Oh, Granny dear, tell us,' the children cried, 'where we
May find the shining Mistletoe that grows upon the tree?'
At length the Dame told them, but cautioned them to mind
To greet the Willow civilly, and leave a bit behind.

'Who cares,' said the children, 'for this old Willow-man?
We'll take the Mistletoe, and he may catch us if he can.'
With rage the ancient Willow shakes in every limb,
For they have taken all, and have not left a bit for him!

Then bright gleamed the holly, the Christmas berries shone,
But in the wintry wind without the Willow-man did moan:
'Ungrateful, and wasteful! The mystic Mistletoe
A hundred years hath grown on me, but never more
    shall grow.'

A year soon passed by, and the children came once more,
But not a sprig of Mistletoe the aged Willow bore.
Each slender spray pointed; he mocked them in his glee,
And chuckled in his wooden heart, that ancient Willow-tree.

Oh, children, who gather the spoils of wood and wold,
From selfish greed and wilful waste your little
    hands withhold.
Though fair things be common, this moral bear in mind,
'Pick thankfully and modestly, and leave a bit behind.'

Juliana Horatia Ewing (1841–85)

When We Went Out With Grandmamma

When we went out with Grandmamma –
    Mamma said for a treat –
Oh, dear, how stiff we had to walk
    As we went down the street.

One on each side we had to go,
    And never laugh or loll;
I carried Prim, her Spaniard dog,
    And Tom, her parasol.

If I looked right, if Tom looked left,
    'Tom, Susan – I'm ashamed;
And little Prim, I'm sure, is shocked,
    To hear such naughties named.'

She said we had no manners,
    If we ever talked or sung;
'You should have seen,' said Grandmamma,
    'Me walk, when I was young.'

She said they never wished them
    To play – oh, indeed!
They learnt to sew and needlework
    Or else to write and read.

She told us – oh, so often –
　　How little girls and boys,
In the good days when she was young,
　　Never made any noise.

She said her mother never let
　　Her speak a word at meals;
'But now,' said Grandmamma, 'you'd think
　　That children's tongues had wheels

'So fast they go – clack, clack, clack, clack;
　　Now listen well, I pray,
And let me see you both improve
　　From what I've said to-day.'

Kate Greenaway (1846–1901)

Dedicatory Poem for 'Underwoods'

To her, for I must still regard her
As feminine in her degree,
Who has been my unkind bombarder
Year after year, in grief and glee,
Year after year, with oaken tree;
And yet betweenwhiles my laudator
In terms astonishing to me –
To the Right Reverend The Spectator
I here, a humble dedicator,
Bring the last apples from my tree.

In tones of love, in tones of warning,
She hailed me through my brief career;
And kiss and buffet, night and morning,
Told me my grandmamma was near;
Whether she praised me high and clear
Through her unrivalled circulation,
Or, sanctimonious insincere,
She damned me with a misquotation –
A chequered but a sweet relation,
Say, was it not, my granny dear?

Believe me, granny, altogether
Yours, though perhaps to your surprise.
Oft have you spruced my wounded feather,
Oft brought a light into my eyes –
For notice still the writer cries.
In any civil age or nation,
The book that is not talked of dies.
So that shall be my termination:
Whether in praise or execration,
Still, if you love me, criticise!

Robert Louis Stevenson (1850–94)

Extract from Good and Bad Children

Children, you are very little,
And your bones are very brittle;
If you would grow great and stately,
You must try to walk sedately.

You must still be bright and quiet,
And content with simple diet;
And remain, through all bewild'ring,
Innocent and honest children.

Happy hearts and happy faces,
Happy play in grassy places –
That was how in ancient ages,
Children grew to kings and sages.

But the unkind and the unruly,
And the sort who eat unduly,
They must never hope for glory –
Theirs is quite a different story!

Robert Louis Stevenson (1850–94)

Little Kids

'Little kids,' you call us
As we are at play.
You were little children
Just the other day.

Now to-morrow nears us,
Soon we too shall stand
Men and women rulers
Of the sea and land.

'Little kids' at play time:
But at home or school
Think about our future,
Make us fit to rule.

Guide us wisely onward,
Teach us what is true.
Though we are but kiddies
We are watching you!

Give us good examples!
While we are at play,
Often we are aping
What you do and say.

Ella Wheeler Wilcox (1850–1919)

Opportunity

Granny's gone a-visitin',
Seen huh git huh shawl
W'en I was a-hidin' down
Hime de gyahden wall.
Seen huh put her bonnet on,
Seen huh tie de strings,
An' I'se gone to dreamin' now
'Bout dem cakes an' t'ings.

On de she'f behime de do' –
Mussy, what a feas'!
Soon ez she gits out o' sight,
I kin eat in peace.
I bin watchin' fu' a week
Des fu' dis hyeah chance.
Mussy, w'en I gits in daih,
I'll des sholy dance.

Lemon pie an' gingah-cake,
Let me set an' t'ink –
Vinegah an' sugah, too,
Dat 'll mek a drink;
Ef dey's one t'ing dat I loves
Mos' pu'ticlahly,
It is eatin' sweet t'ings an'
A-drinkin' Sangaree.

Lawdy, won' po' granny raih
W'en she see de she'f;
W'en I t'ink erbout huh face,
I's mos' 'shamed myse'f.
Well, she gone, an' hyeah I is,
Back behime de do' –
Look hyeah! Gran' 's done 'spected me,
Dain't no sweets no mo'.

Evah sweet is hid erway,
Job des done up brown;
Pusson t'ink dat someun t'ought
Dey was t'eves erroun';
Dat des breaks my heart in two,
Oh how bad I feel!
Des to t'ink my own gramma
B'lieved dat I 'u'd steal!

Paul Laurence Dunbar (1872–1906)

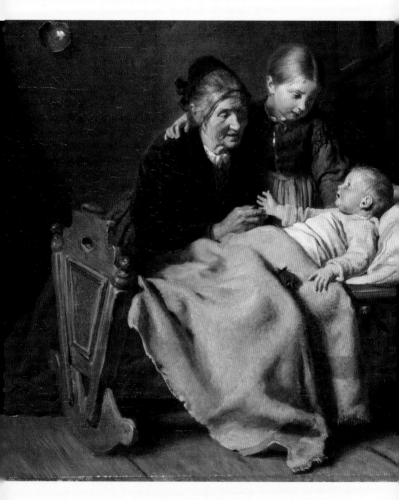

Ever the Pupil

Teach me. Teach me!
Let me never become so old
That my ears are not pits.
Teach me. Teach me!
Let every man become my teacher.
Let every sorrow speak deeply.
Let every joy inscribe me.
Teach me. Teach me!
For if I stop listening,
I shall stop forever!
Yea, the writing of the ages
Speaks Eternity as ever
Listening, ever waiting.
Teach me. Teach me!
Let me ne'er forget that I am a child;
That tomorrow is a secret,
A joyful secret, not yet imparted;
That Yesterday was a plaything
Which I loved, but left
Upon a pathway within a shadow.
Teach me. Teach me –
That I am a little child!
Let me be forever learning,
Ne'er forever yearning!

Patience Worth (1883–1937)

Wisdom

When I have ceased to break my wings
Against the faultiness of things,
And learned that compromises wait
Behind each hardly opened gate,
When I have looked Life in the eyes,
Grown calm and very coldly wise,
Life will have given me the Truth,
And taken in exchange—my youth.

Sara Teasdale (1884–1933)

Child, Child

Child, child, love while you can
The voice and the eyes and the soul of a man;
Never fear though it break your heart –
Out of the wound new joy will start;
Only love proudly and gladly and well,
Though love be heaven or love be hell.

Child, child, love while you may,
For life is short as a happy day;
Never fear the thing you feel –
Only by love is life made real;
Love, for the deadly sins are seven,
Only through love will you enter heaven.

Sara Teasdale (1884–1933)

Sixty to Sixteen

If I were young as you, Sixteen,
   And you were old as I,
I would not be as I have been,
   You would not be so shy –
We should not watch with careless mien
   The golden days go by,
If I were young as you, Sixteen,
   And you were old as I.

The years of youth are yours, Sixteen;
   Such years of old had I,
But time has set his seal between
   Dark eyebrow and dark eye.
Sere grow the leaves that once were green,
   The song turns to a sigh:
Ah! very young are you, Sixteen,
   And very old am I.

Red bloom-times come and go, Sixteen,
    With snow-soft feet, but I
Shall be no more as I have been
    In times of bloom gone by;
For dimmer grows the pleasant scene
    Beneath the pleasant sky;
The world is growing old, Sixteen –
    The weary world and I.

Ah, would that once again, Sixteen,
    A kissing mouth had I;
The days would gaily go, I ween,
    Though death should stand anigh,
If springtime's green were evergreen,
    If Love would never die,
And I were young as you, Sixteen,
    And you were old as I.

Victor James Daley (1858–1905)

A Few Rules for Beginners

Babies must not eat the coal
And they must not make grimaces,
Nor in party dresses roll
And must never black their faces.

They must learn that pointing's rude,
They must sit quite still at table,
And must always eat the food
Put before them, if they're able.

If they fall, they must not cry,
Though it's known how painful this is;
No – there's always Mother by
Who will comfort them with kisses.

Katherine Mansfield (1888–1923)

MEMORIES

Rose Barton

Extract from To Memory

Hail, Memory! Whose magic pow'r
Can gild the present gloomy hour
With the gay colours of the past,
Can smooth the wrinkled brow of age,
The pangs of absence can assuage,
And bid love's fleeting transports last!
At dawn of life's tempestuous day,
Ere reason had assum'd the sway,
Ere passion's mingled storm arose,
Thou deign'dst before mine infant eyes,
As yet unskill'd the boon to prize,
Thy golden treasures to disclose.
At length, enrich'd, by thee I wove,
(Soaring the vulgar throng above)
Fair garlands for the shrine of truth.
O, may I long thy favour share
Ere all-destroying time impair
The generous gifts bestow'd in youth.

Yon gorgeous palace! Solemn fane!
Yon floating castle on the main!
To whose providing owe we these?
Could art her lofty fabrics build,
Should bounteous nature cease to yield
Her marbles bright, her towering trees?
And what would fancy's powers avail
If all thy treasur'd stores should fail,
Sav'd in the dark eclipse of time?
Rich stores of action! Passion, thought!

Short joys, by long repentance bought!
And grov'ling vice, and worth sublime.
Without thee, mute the living lyre;
Though touch'd by Phoebus' hallow'd fire,
Silent the tuneful poet's tongue;
On thee, the brave for fame rely;
Unsung without thee, patriots die;
And god-like heroes bleed unsung.
Even life itself to thee we owe,
Thou canst the wond'rous charm bestow
To stop the moments as they fly;

And but for thee, they fleet so fast,
(Yet hardly present when they're past)
That man with every breath would die.
O stay, and soothe my sorrows still,
A motley life of good and ill
Was mine, is every mortal's fate;
But I have known long years of bliss,
O, let me still remember this,
Though widow'd now, and desolate.
Ah! No, for me no balm hast thou,
A widow'd, childless father now!
And grief my earthly, endless doom.
Yet hope still lives beyond the grave;
God surely tries us but to save!
They beckon me; I come! I come!

Joanna Baillie (1762–1851)

The Grandmother

And Willy, my eldest-born, is gone, you say, little Anne?
Ruddy and white, and strong on his legs, he looks like a man.
And Willy's wife has written: she never was over-wise,
Never the wife for Willy: he would n't take my advice.

For, Annie, you see, her father was not the man to save,
Had n't a head to manage, and drank himself into his grave.
Pretty enough, very pretty! But I was against it for one.
Eh! But he would n't hear me – and Willy, you say, is gone.

Willy, my beauty, my eldest-born, the flower of the flock;
Never a man could fling him: for Willy stood like a rock.
'Here's a leg for a babe of a week!' says doctor; and he
    would be bound,
There was not his like that year in twenty parishes round.

Strong of his hands, and strong on his legs, but still of
    his tongue!
I ought to have gone before him: I wonder he went so young.
I cannot cry for him, Annie: I have not long to stay;
Perhaps I shall see him the sooner, for he lived far away.

Why do you look at me, Annie? You think I am hard and cold;
But all my children have gone before me, I am so old:
I cannot weep for Willy, nor can I weep for the rest;
Only at your age, Annie, I could have wept with the best.

For I remember a quarrel I had with your father, my dear,
All for a slanderous story, that cost me many a tear.
I mean your grandfather, Annie: it cost me a world of woe,
Seventy years ago, my darling, seventy years ago.

For Jenny, my cousin, had come to the place, and I knew
    right well
That Jenny had tript in her time: I knew, but I would not tell.
And she to be coming and slandering me, the base little liar!
But the tongue is a fire as you know, my dear, the tongue
    is a fire.

And the parson made it his text that week, and he
    said likewise,
That a lie which is half a truth is ever the blackest of lies,
That a lie which is all a lie may be met and fought
    with outright,
But a lie which is part a truth is a harder matter to fight.

And Willy had not been down to the farm for a week
    and a day;
And all things look'd half-dead, tho' it was the middle of May.
Jenny, to slander me, who knew what Jenny had been!
But soiling another, Annie, will never make oneself clean.

And I cried myself well-nigh blind, and all of an evening late
I climb'd to the top of the garth, and stood by the road
    at the gate.
The moon like a rick on fire was rising over the dale,
And whit, whit, whit, in the bush beside me chirrupt
    the nightingale.

All of a sudden he stopt: there past by the gate of the farm,
Willy – he did n't see me – and Jenny hung on his arm.
Out into the road I started, and spoke I scarce knew how;
Ah, there's no fool like the old one – it makes me angry now.

Willy stood up like a man, and look'd the thing that he meant;
Jenny, the viper, made me a mocking courtesy and went.
And I said, 'Let us part: in a hundred years it'll all be
    the same,
You cannot love me at all, if you love not my good name.'

And he turn'd, and I saw his eyes all wet, in the
    sweet moonshine:
Sweetheart, I love you so well that your good name is mine.
And what do I care for Jane, let her speak of you well of ill;
But marry me out of hand: we two shall be happy still.'

'Marry you, Willy!' said I, 'but I needs must speak my mind,
And I fear you'll listen to tales, be jealous and hard and unkind.'
But he turn'd and claspt me in his arms, and answer'd,
    'No, love, no;'
Seventy years ago, my darling, seventy years ago.

So Willy and I were wedded: I wore a lilac gown;
And the ringers rang with a will, and he gave the ringers
    a crown.
But the first that ever I bare was dead before he was born,
Shadow and shine is life, little Annie, flower and thorn.

That was the first time, too, that ever I thought of death.
There lay the sweet little body that never had drawn a breath.
I had not wept, little Anne, not since I had been a wife;
But I wept like a child that day, for the babe had fought for
    his life.

His dear little face was troubled, as if with anger or pain:
I look'd at the still little body – his trouble had all been
    in vain.
For Willy I cannot weep, I shall see him another morn:
But I wept like a child for the child that was dead before
    he was born.

But he cheer'd me, my good man, for he seldom said me nay:
Kind, like a man, was he; like a man, too, would have his way:
Never jealous – not he: we had many a happy year;
And he died, and I could not weep – my own time seem'd so near.

But I wish'd it had been God's will that I, too, then could
     have died:
I began to be tired a little, and fain had slept at his side.
And that was ten years back, or more, if I don't forget:
But as to the children, Annie, they're all about me yet.

Pattering over the boards, my Annie who left me at two,
Patter she goes, my own little Annie, an Annie like you:
Pattering over the boards, she comes and goes at her will,
While Harry is in the five-acre and Charlie ploughing the hill.

And Harry and Charlie, I hear them too – they sing to
    their team:
Often they come to the door in a pleasant kind of a dream.
They come and sit by my chair, they hover about my bed –
I am not always certain if they be alive or dead.

And yet I know for a truth, there's none of them left alive;
For Harry went at sixty, your father at sixty-five:
And Willy, my eldest born, at nigh threescore and ten;
I knew them all as babies, and now they're elderly men.

For mine is a time of peace, it is not often I grieve;
I am oftener sitting at home in my father's farm at eve:
And the neighbours come and laugh and gossip, and so do I;
I find myself often laughing at things that have long gone by.

To be sure the preacher says, our sins should make us sad:
But mine is a time of peace, and there is Grace to be had;
And God, not man, is the Judge of us all when life shall cease;
And in this Book, little Annie, the message is one of Peace

And age is a time of peace, so it be free from pain,
And happy has been my life; but I would not live it again.
I seem to be tired a little, that's all, and long for rest;
Only at your age, Annie, I could have wept with the best.

So Willy has gone, my beauty, my eldest-born, my flower;
But how can I weep for Willy, he has but gone for an hour –
Gone for a minute, my son, from this room into the next;
I, too, shall go in a minute. What time have I to be vext?

And Willy's wife has written, she never was over-wise.
Get me my glasses, Annie: thank God that I keep my eyes.
There is but a trifle left you, when I shall have past away.
But stay with the old woman now: you cannot have long
    to stay.

Lord Alfred Tennyson (1809–92)

No Time Like the Old Time

There is no time like the old time, when you and I were young,
When the buds of April blossomed, and the birds of spring-time sung!
The garden's brightest glories by summer suns are nursed,
But oh, the sweet, sweet violets, the flowers that opened first!

There is no place like the old place, where you and I were born,
Where we lifted first our eyelids on the splendors of the morn
From the milk-white breast that warmed us, from the clinging
    arms that bore,
Where the dear eyes glistened o'er us that will look on us no more!

There is no friend like the old friend, who has shared our
    morning days,
No greeting like his welcome, no homage like his praise
Fame is the scentless sunflower, with gaudy crown of gold;
But friendship is the breathing rose, with sweets in every fold.

There is no love like the old love, that we courted in our pride;
Though our leaves are falling, falling, and we're fading side by side
There are blossoms all around us with the colours of our dawn,
And we live in borrowed sunshine when the day-star
   is withdrawn.

There are no times like the old times, they shall never be forgot!
There is no place like the old place, keep green the dear old spot!
There are no friends like our old friends, may Heaven prolong
   their lives
There are no loves like our old loves, God bless our loving wives!

Oliver Wendell Holmes Snr (1809–94)

The Old Man Dreams

Oh for one hour of youthful joy!
Give back my twentieth spring!
I'd rather laugh, a bright-haired boy,
Than reign, a grey-beard king.

Off with the spoils of wrinkled age!
Away with Learning's crown!
Tear out life's Wisdom-written page,
And dash its trophies down!

One moment let my life-blood stream
From boyhood's fount of flame!
Give me one giddy, reeling dream
Of life all love and fame!

My listening angel heard the prayer,
And, calmly smiling, said,
'If I but touch thy silvered hair
Thy hasty wish hath sped.

'But is there nothing in thy track,
To bid thee fondly stay,
While the swift seasons hurry back
To find the wished-for day?'

'Ah, truest soul of womankind!
Without thee what were life?
One bliss I cannot leave behind:
I'll take my precious wife!'

The angel took a sapphire pen
And wrote in rainbow dew,
The man would be a boy again,
And be a husband too!

'And is there nothing yet unsaid,
Before the change appears?
Remember, all their gifts have fled
With those dissolving years.'

'Why, yes'; for memory would recall
My fond paternal joys;
'I could not bear to leave them all –
I'll take my girl and boys.'

The smiling angel dropped his pen –
'Why, this will never do;
The man would be a boy again,
And be a father too!'

And so I laughed – my laughter woke
The household with its noise –
And wrote my dream, when morning broke,
To please the grey-haired boys.

Oliver Wendell Holmes Snr (1809–94)

Evening Solace

The human heart has hidden treasures,
In secret kept, in silence sealed;
The thoughts, the hopes, the dreams, the pleasures,
Whose charms were broken if revealed.
And days may pass in gay confusion,
And nights in rosy riot fly,
While, lost in Fame's or Wealth's illusion,
The memory of the Past may die.

But, there are hours of lonely musing,
Such as in evening silence come,
When, soft as birds their pinions closing,
The heart's best feelings gather home.
Then in our souls there seems to languish
A tender grief that is not woe;
And thoughts that once wrung groans of anguish,
Now cause but some mild tears to flow.

And feelings, once as strong as passions,
Float softly back a faded dream;
Our own sharp griefs and wild sensations,
The tale of others' sufferings seem.
Oh! When the heart is freshly bleeding,
How longs it for that time to be,
When, through the mist of years receding,
Its woes but live in reverie!

And it can dwell on moonlight glimmer,
On evening shade and loneliness;
And, while the sky grows dim and dimmer,
Feel no untold and strange distress
Only a deeper impulse given
By lonely hour and darkened room,
To solemn thoughts that soar to heaven,
Seeking a life and world to come.

Charlotte Bronte (1816–55)

The Old Crib

I know thou art a senseless thing,
Still recollections round thee cling
Of joys long past;
And I would fain retain thee now,
Yet want's stern hand and lowering brow
Has o'er me cast
His misery with weight untold,
And, much prized crib, thou must be sold!
Ah! Well do I remember yet,
Remember? Can I well forget
That happy day,
When a swift tide my spirit moved,
And with a mother's soul, I loved
The child that lay
Within thy lap-my precious boy!
How throbbed my heart with untold joy.
How swiftly, then, the years sweep on,
With love, joy, wealth, they come, are gone,
And very soon
A little dark-eyed, bonny girl,
Pressed on thy pillow many a curl.

Most precious boon
That ever was to mortal given –
A cherub, from the gates of heaven.
And yet again, some powerful spell,
Called to this earth, sweet baby Bell,
My sunbeam child,
With hair of gold, and eyes of blue,
And cheeks that vie the rosebud's hue –
Pure, undefiled!
About my heart she seems to twine,
As round the oak, the clinging vine.
Take back thy gold! It shall not go!
'Twas mine in weal, and now in woe:
It comforts me.
It takes me back, in fitful gleams,
To the sweet, fairy land of dreams,
And then I see
Those little heads, with glossy curls,
My manly boy, my little girls!

Mary Eliza Perine Tucker Lambert (1838–1958)

The Burial in the Snow

How well do I remember
   Of a burial in the snow,
On a winter's evening
   Some fifteen years ago;
The ground was covered over
   With the beautiful crystal snow,
And it glistened in the moonlight,
   Like diamonds all aglow.

It was a pleasant evening,
   That merry Christmas eve;
And I never can forget, how
   The frost hung on the tree.
The moon was shining clearly,
   And the sleigh-bells rang so sweet;
Ah, it was splendid sleighing,
   The snow was two feet deep.

My grandparents were living
   Some two miles then away,
My parents went to see them,
   To spend the holiday.
I went with my kind parents,
   For the evening was sublime,
To see dear aunts and uncles,
   And have a merry time,

I saw the beaming faces
  Of my grandparents dear,
As they met us on the door-step,
  With welcome words of cheer.
In fancy I can see them
  As in the days of yore,
When they welcome home their children
  Through the old familiar door.

The banquet board that evening,
  Was filled with cake and wine,
Delicious fruits and oysters
  That came from foreign clime.
It was a merry party
  That met once more to roam,
My grandparents were happy,
  Their children were all home.

Grandpapa said, 'dear children,
  Lay the tea things aside,
And some of you get ready
  To take a pleasant ride.
The moon is shining clearly,
  The evening is sublime,
O'er the crystal snow we'll glide,
  And have a jolly time.'

Hats and cloaks were soon put on,
    By those who wish to go,
They were wrapped up snug and warm,
    For a sleigh ride o'er the snow. Their hearts were lig
    and gleeful,
    They rode away with ease,
I never can forget them,
    Or that merry Christmas eve.

On that beautiful evening,
    They rode five miles away,
O'er hills, and dales, and frozen snow,
    With prospects bright and gay.
They came to their journey's end,
    And soon were homeward bound,
A more joyous, happy band
    Was nowhere to be found,

The merry sleigh bells ringing
    Out on the midnight air,
And merry voices singing
    All 'right side up with care!'
The horses were high-spirited,
    They ran away, and lo!
Broke loose from the sleigh, and left
    It buried in the snow.

The people of that party
  Lay scattered all around,
Some were frightened, others laughed,
  To think it happened so,
That the end of their sleigh ride
  Was a burial in the snow.

Yet they were gay and happy,
  The bright moon o'er them shone,
And laughing o'er their sleigh ride,
  They all went trudging home.
Some of those friends are dead and gone,
  That met in that old home,
And never will we meet again,
  Around that dear hearth stone.

Julia A. Moore (1847–1920)

My Native Home

My native home why did I roam
From thy dear sheltering bowers?
Where birds and bees sang mid the trees,
Through the long summer hours.

That cottage brown not build in town,
But in the country glade,
Where laughing brook with many a crook
Played 'neath the willows' shade.

That old brick mill upon the hill,
The brooklet running by;
Down in that brook with line and hook,
To catch the fish we'd try.

The watchdog gray slept on the hay,
The cat played with her kitten,
And Grandma Squire sat by the fire,
So busy with her knitting.

Then after tea so merrily
Around the fire we'd come,
O grandma dear, we want to hear,
A story, please, just one.

All this I know was long ago,
But still I well remember
The walnut shade down in the glade
And beachnuts in November.

Child of today, enjoy your play
Through meadows red with clover.
For brooklets rare will echo there,
A wish to be a rover.

And when you roam far, far from home,
And have a moment's leisure,
You'll wish like me that home to see,
Where days brought naught but pleasure.

Nettie Squire Sutton (19th century)

Waiting

I can't believe my wedding day was fifty years ago!
This is the second day of March! The clock is ticking slow;
The sun shines in across the room. Just see the folks go by!
I can't remember half of them who nod so pleasantly.

The little English sparrows flit in the lilac bush outside;
I like to watch the busy things. There's one that's tried and tried
To break a string the children tied around a branch one day;
How hard he pulls it with his beak! Now he has flown away.

So it was fifty years ago! It doesn't seem so long.
I've felt my age more this last year, and yet I'm pretty strong.
I don't do much about the house, but still I know what's done;
I know as well what's going on as Jane or any one.

Jane frets me dreadfully sometimes and yet she's always kind.
She helps me when there is no need and has me on her mind;
She needn't think I'm past all use or that I'm like to fall;
I've never missed my footing yet, though I'm so old and all.

But things don't seem to take my mind that happen nowadays.
I like the folks I used to know; I keep old-fashioned ways;
I read the Psalms and Book of John and find them always new;
And I can knit, but I can't sew same as I used to do.

The young folks think they understand just how to manage life;
We old folks pity them; we've learnt its change and loss and strife.
Life is a fight I tell you plain, it doesn't come to hand
Just as you want to have it come or just as you have planned.

If you'd foretold me how it's been through all these fifty years
I should have been discouraged and had no lack of fears,
And wished I could lie down and die, but somehow I've
     had strength
That's come to me with every day all through my whole
     life's length.

I started fair my wedding day, for my dear man was kind
And always pleasant spoken; we were mostly of a mind.
Of course we had our failings out but nothing that would last;
It always was my fault, for I was young and spoke too fast.

And John, you see, was older by some ten years than I.
At first I was afraid of him when we kept company.
He was a sort of man on whom you felt you could depend,
But very quiet in his ways. His mother was a Friend.

My hardest time was when he died. It seemed to me 'twas wrong
The Lord should take him out of life and let me drag along
As best I could, with little means and all my children small,
Just when we seemed to see our way and get ahead at all.

But God knows best. If it had been my life had suited me
If I had had an easy time, and not known poverty,
I should have been a flighty thing without a bit of sense.
I turned my hand to everything – to knit or build a fence.

There weren't the folks to call on then that I could get to-day,
For help was scarce, the farms were few, and I'd no means to pay.
I went to work with all my might and tried my home to keep,
But I can tell you many a night I've cried myself to sleep.

I know the Lord has prospered me. I've done the best I could,
And I've stood in my lot and place as anybody should.
The farm-land some folks would have sold I held, because I knew
Some day 'twould be good property, and all my hopes come true.

I've parted with it piece by piece – you see the town has grown,
Just as John always said it would. If other folks had known
And had the foresight that he had! Instead of that they told
How I should never get along unless the farm was sold.

My boys grew fast and soon took hold, and then my way
    was plain,
For all the money they had cost they soon brought back again;
And like a busy hive of bees we were from morn till night;
We had our health, the Lord be thanked! And that made work
    seem light.

The children all have settled down in good homes of their own,
Excepting Jane, and but for her I should be left alone;
She had her chances too, but then she's not the marrying kind;
I couldn't do without her now, I'm glad she stayed behind.

I'm glad I'm mistress of my house; the children often say
I must break up, that Jane and I were better off to stay
With some of them, for I'm so old and Jane's not over strong;
But I won't listen to their plans; I've made my own too long.

My life seems like a book that's read and put up on the shelf;
I used to be a-hurrying round; I don't feel like myself;
Sometimes I'm tired of keeping still, I want to be at work;
I see so many things to do and I don't like to shirk.

I used to have to toil and plan, and now I have to wait,
And I suppose I mustn't fret, but in a future state
I shall be sure to find my place and be some use again,
For there we still shall serve the Lord – the Scripture says it plain.

So it's my golden wedding day, though we have been apart
For forty years, and yet John knows that he has kept my heart,
And I know that he looks for me and waits for me to come;
I've tried to do the best I could – and here or there it's home!

Sarah Orne Jewett (1849–1909)

Old Man's Nursery Rhyme

I
In the jolly winters
    Of the long-ago,
It was not so cold as now?
    O! No! No!
Then, as I remember,
    Snowballs, to eat,
Were as good as apples now,
    And every bit as sweet!

II
In the jolly winters
    Of the dead-and-gone,
Bub was warm as summer,
    With his red mitts on –
Just in his little waist,
    And-pants all together,
Who ever heard him growl
    About cold weather?

III
In the jolly winters
    Of the long-ago,
Was it half so cold as now?
    O! No! No!
Who caught his death o' cold,
    Making prints of men
Flat-backed in snow that now's
    Twice as cold again?

IV
In the jolly winters
   Of the dead-and-gone,
Startin' out rabbit-hunting
   Early as the dawn –
Who ever froze his fingers,
   Ears, heels, or toes,
Or'd a cared if he had?
   Nobody knows!

V
Nights by the kitchen-stove,
   Shelling white and red
Corn in the skillet, and
   Sleepin' four abed!
Ah! The jolly winters
   Of the long-ago!
We were not so old as now –
   O! No! No!

James Whitcomb Riley (1849–1916)

Grandfather Squeers

'My grandfather Squeers,' said The Raggedy Man,
As he solemnly lighted his pipe and began –

'The most indestructible man, for his years,
And the grandest on earth, was my grandfather Squeers!

'He said, when he rounded his three-score-and-ten,
"I've the hang of it now and can do it again!"

'He had frozen his heels so repeatedly, he
Could tell by them just what the weather would be;

'And would laugh and declare, "while the Almanac would
Most falsely prognosticate, he never could!"

'Such a hale constitution had grandfather Squeers
That, 'though he'd used "navy" for sixty odd years,

'He still chewed a dime's-worth six days of the week,
While the seventh he passed with a chew in each cheek:

'Then my grandfather Squeers had a singular knack
Of sitting around on the small of his back,

'With his legs like a letter Y stretched o'er the grate
Wherein 'twas his custom to ex-pec-tor-ate.

'He was fond of tobacco in manifold ways,
And would sit on the door-step, of sunshiny days,

'And smoke leaf-tobacco he'd raised strictly for
The pipe he'd used all through The Mexican War.'

And The Raggedy Man said, refilling the bowl
Of his own pipe and leisurely picking a coal

From the stove with his finger and thumb, 'You can see
What a tee-nacious habit he's fastened on me!

'And my grandfather Squeers took a special delight
In pruning his corns every Saturday night

'With a horn-handled razor, whose edge he excused
By saying 'twas one that his grandfather used;

'And, though deeply etched in the haft of the same
Was the ever-euphonious Wostenholm's name,

'Twas my grandfather's custom to boast of the blade
As "A Seth Thomas razor – the best ever made!"

'No Old Settlers' Meeting, or Pioneers' Fair,
Was complete without grandfather Squeers in the chair

'To lead off the programme by telling folks how
"He used to shoot deer where the Court-House stands now"

'How 'he felt, of a truth, to live over the past,
When the country was wild and unbroken and vast,

'That the little log cabin was just plenty fine
For himself, his companion, and fambly of nine!

'When they didn't have even a pump, or a tin,
But drunk surface-water, year out and year in,

'From the old-fashioned gourd that was sweeter, by odds,
Than the goblets of gold at the lips of the gods!'

Then The Raggedy Man paused to plaintively say
It was clockin' along to'rds the close of the day –

And he'd ought to get back to his work on the lawn, –
Then dreamily blubbered his pipe and went on:

'His teeth were imperfect – my grandfather owned
That he couldn't eat oysters unless they were "boned";

'And his eyes were so weak, and so feeble of sight,
He couldn't sleep with them unless, every night,

'He put on his spectacles – all he possessed –
Three pairs – with his goggles on top of the rest.

'And my grandfather always, retiring at night,
Blew down the lamp-chimney to put out the light;

'Then he'd curl up on edge like a shaving, in bed,
And puff and smoke pipes in his sleep, it is said:

'And would snore oftentimes as the legends relate,
Till his folks were wrought up to a terrible state –

'Then he'd snort, and rear up, and roll over; and there,
In the subsequent hush they could hear him chew air.

'And so glaringly bald was the top of his head
That many's the time he has musingly said,

'As his eyes journeyed o'er its reflex in the glass –
"I must set out a few signs of 'Keep Off the Grass!'"

'So remarkably deaf was my grandfather Squeers
That he had to wear lightning-rods over his ears

'To even hear thunder – and oftentimes then
He was forced to request it to thunder again.'

James Whitcomb Riley (1849–1916)

A Valentine

Your gran'ma, in her youth, was quite
   As blithe a little maid as you.
And, though her hair is snowy white,
   Her eyes still have their maiden blue,
And on her cheeks, as fair as thine,
   Methinks a girlish blush would glow
If she recalled the valentine

She got, ah! Many years ago.
A valorous youth loved gran'ma then,
    And wooed her in that auld lang syne;
And first he told his secret when
    He sent the maid that valentine.
No perfumed page nor sheet of gold
    Was that first hint of love he sent,
But with the secret gran'pa told –
    'I love you' – gran'ma was content.

Go, ask your gran'ma, if you will,
    If, though her head be bowed and gray,
If, though her feeble pulse be chill,
    True love abideth not for aye;
By that quaint portrait on the wall,
    That smiles upon her from above,
Methinks your gran'ma can recall
    The sweet divinity of love.

Dear Elsie, here's no page of gold –
    No sheet embossed with cunning art –
But here's a solemn pledge of old:
    'I love you, love, with all my heart.'
And if in what I send you here
    You read not all of love expressed,
Go – go to gran'ma, Elsie dear,
    And she will tell you all the rest!

Eugene Field (1850–95)

Extract from Grandpa's Christmas

In his great cushioned chair by the fender
An old man sits dreaming to-night,
His withered hands, licked by the tender,
Warm rays of the red anthracite,
Are folded before him, all listless;
His dim eyes are fixed on the blaze,
While over him sweeps the resistless
Flood-tide of old days.

He hears not the mirth in the hallway,
He hears not the sounds of good cheer,
That through the old homestead ring alway
In the glad Christmas-time of the year.
He heeds not the chime of sweet voices
As the last gifts are hung on the tree.
In a long-vanished day he rejoices –
In his lost 'used to be'.

He has gone back across dead Decembers
To his childhood's fair land of delight;
And his mother's sweet smile he remembers,
As he hangs up his stocking at night.
He remembers the dream-haunted slumber
All broken and restless because
Of the visions that came without number
Of dear Santa Claus.

Again, in his manhood's beginning,
He sees himself thrown on the world,
And into the vortex of sinning
By Pleasure's strong arms he is hurled.
He hears the sweet Christmas bells ringing,
'Repent ye, repent ye, and pray;'
But he joins with his comrades in singing
A bacchanal lay.

Again he stands under the holly
With a blushing face lifted to his;
For love has been stronger than folly,
And has turned him from vice unto bliss;
And the whole world is lit with new glory
As the sweet vows are uttered again,
While the Christmas bells tell the old story
Of peace unto men.

Again, with his little brood 'round him,
He sits by the fair mother-wife;
He knows that the angels have crowned him
With the truest, best riches of life;
And the hearts of the children, untroubled,
Are filled with the gay Christmas-tide;

Ella Wheeler Wilcox (1850–1919)

The Old School List

In a wild moraine of forgotten books,
On the glacier of years gone by,
As I plied my rake for order's sake,
There was one that caught my eye:
And I sat by the shelf till I lost myself.
And roamed in the crowded mist,
And heard lost voices and saw lost looks,
As I pored on an Old School List.

What a jumble of names! There were some that I knew,
As a brother is known: to-day
Gone I know not where, nay I hardly care,
For their places are full: and, they –
What climes they have ranged: how much they're changed!
Time, place and pursuits assist
In transforming them: stay where you are: adieu!
You are all in the Old School List.

There are some who did nothing at school, much since:
And others much then, since naught:
They are middle-aged men, grown bald since then:
Some have travelled, and some have fought:
And some have written, and some are bitten
With strange new faiths: desist
From tracking them: broker or priest of prince,
They are all in the Old School List.

There's a grave grey lawyer in King's Bench Walk,
Whose clients are passing few:
He seldom speaks: in those lonely weeks,
What on earth can he find to do?
Well, he stroked the eight – what a splendid fate!
And the Newcastle barely missed:
'A future Lord Chancellor!' so we'd talk
In the days of the Old School List.

There were several duffers and several bores,
Whose faces I've half forgot,
Whom I lived among, when the world was young,
And who talked 'no end of rot':
Are they now little clerks who stroll in the Parks
Or scribble with grimy fist,
Or rich little peers who hire Scotch moors?
Well – they're all in the Old School List.

There were some who were certain to prosper and thrive,
And certain to do no more,
Who were 'capital chaps,' and, tho' moderate saps,
Would never stay in after four:
Now day after day they are packed away,
After being connubially kissed,
To work in the city from ten to five:
There they are in the Old School List.

There were two good fellows I used to know.
How distant it all appears!
We played together in football weather,
And messed together for years:
Now one of them's wed, and the other's dead
So long that he's hardly missed
Save by us, who messed with him years ago:
But we're all in the Old School List.

James Kenneth Stephen (1859–92)

THE PASSAGE OF TIME

The Grey Hair

One day I observed a grey hair in my head;
I plucked it right out, when it thus to me said:
'You may smile, if you wish, at your treatment of me,
But a score of my friends soon will make a mockery of you.'

Yehudah Halevi (1075–1141)

All the World's a Stage
From As You Like It, Act 2, Scene 7

All the world's a stage,
And all the men and women merely players;
They have their exits and their entrances,
And one man in his time plays many parts,
His acts being seven ages. At first, the infant,
Mewling and puking in the nurse's arms.
Then the whining schoolboy, with his satchel
And shining morning face, creeping like snail
Unwillingly to school. And then the lover,
Sighing like furnace, with a woeful ballad
Made to his mistress' eyebrow. Then a soldier,
Full of strange oaths and bearded like the pard,
Jealous in honor, sudden and quick in quarrel,
Seeking the bubble reputation

Even in the cannon's mouth. And then the justice,
In fair round belly with good capon lined,
With eyes severe and beard of formal cut,
Full of wise saws and modern instances;
And so he plays his part. The sixth age shifts
Into the lean and slippered pantaloon,
With spectacles on nose and pouch on side;
His youthful hose, well saved, a world too wide
For his shrunk shank, and his big manly voice,
Turning again toward childish treble, pipes
And whistles in his sound. Last scene of all,
That ends this strange eventful history,
Is second childishness and mere oblivion,
Sans teeth, sans eyes, sans taste, sans everything.

William Shakespeare (1564–1616)

On Time
Addressed to a Lady on her 84th Birthday

Time sooth, since Time has been, has still sustain'd
The varied murmurs of each wayward mood,
Of tedious pace, of hasty flight arraign'd,
His loss lamented and his influence woo'd.
How is it, favour'd Lady, that on thee
This blighting power no rugged mark has shed?
But traces still, with fairest courtesy,
His gentle progress o'er thy silver'd head?
No vain regrets to thy remembrance cling,
No ill-spent hours thy tranquil mind appal,
Nor would'st thou wish to check his rapid wing,
Or transient joys of scenes long past recal.
Then tell the gay who bask in youthful prime,
Time honours thee, for thou hast honoured Time.

Joanna Baillie (1762–1851)

The Human Seasons

Four seasons fill the measure of the year;
There are four seasons in the mind of man:
He has his lusty Spring, when fancy clear
Takes in all beauty with an easy span:
He has his Summer, when luxuriously
Spring's honey'd cud of youthful thought he loves
To ruminate, and by such dreaming high
Is nearest unto heaven: quiet coves
His soul has in its Autumn, when his wings
He furleth close; contented so to look
On mists in idleness – to let fair things
Pass by unheeded as a threshold brook.
He has his Winter too of pale misfeature,
Or else he would forego his mortal nature.

John Keats (1795–1821)

The Archbishop and Gil Blas

I don't think I feel much older; I'm aware I'm rather gray,
But so are many young folks; I meet 'em every day.
I confess I'm more particular in what I eat and drink,
But one's taste improves with culture; that is all it means, I think.

'Can you read as once you used to?' Well, the printing is so bad,
No young folks' eyes can read it like the books that once we had.
'Are you quite as quick of hearing?' Please to say that once again.
'Don't I use plain words, your Reverence?' Yes, I often use a cane,

But it's not because I need it – no, I always liked a stick;
And as one might lean upon it, 't is as well it should be thick.
Oh, I'm smart, I'm spry, I'm lively – I can walk, yes, that I can,
On the days I feel like walking, just as well as you, young man!

'Don't you get a little sleepy after dinner every day?'
Well, I doze a little, sometimes, but that always was my way.
'Don't you cry a little easier than some twenty years ago?'
Well, my heart is very tender, but I think 't was always so.

'Don't you find it sometimes happens that you can't recall a name?'
Yes, I know such lots of people – but my memory's not to blame.
What! You think my memory's failing! Why, it's just as bright
    and clear,
I remember my great-grandma! She's been dead these sixty year!

'Is your voice a little trembly?' Well, it may be, now and then,
But I write as well as ever with a good old-fashioned pen;
It's the Gillotts make the trouble – not at all my finger-ends –
That is why my hand looks shaky when I sign for dividends.

'Don't you stoop a little, walking?' It's a way I've always had,
I have always been round-shouldered, ever since I was a lad.
'Don't you hate to tie your shoe-strings?' Yes, I own it – that is true.
'Don't you tell old stories over?' I am not aware I do.

'Don't you stay at home of evenings? Don't you love a cushioned seat
In a corner, by the fireside, with your slippers on your feet?
Don't you wear warm fleecy flannels? Don't you muffle up
    your throat
Don't you like to have one help you when you're putting on your coat?

'Don't you like old books you've dogs-eared, you can't
   remember when?
Don't you call it late at nine o'clock and go to bed at ten?
How many cronies can you count of all you used to know
Who called you by your Christian name some fifty years ago?

'How look the prizes to you that used to fire your brain?
You've reared your mound–how high is it above the level plain?
You've drained the brimming golden cup that made your fancy reel,
You've slept the giddy potion off – now tell us how you feel!

'You've watched the harvest ripening till every stem was cropped,
You've seen the rose of beauty fade till every petal dropped,
You've told your thought, you've done your task, you've tracked
   your dial round,'
I backing down! Thank Heaven, not yet! I'm hale and brisk
   and sound,

And good for many a tussle, as you shall live to see;
My shoes are not quite ready yet – don't think you're rid of me!
Old Parr was in his lusty prime when he was older far,
And where will you be if I live to beat old Thomas Parr?

'Ah well, I know, at every age life has a certain charm –
You're going? Come, permit me, please, I beg you'll take my arm.'
I take your arm! Why take your arm? I'd thank you to be told
I'm old enough to walk alone, but not so very old!

Oliver Wendell Holmes Snr (1809–94)

The Song of Seventy

I am not old – I cannot be old,
Though threescore years and ten
Have wasted away, like a tale that is told,
The lives of other men:

I am not old; though friends and foes
Alike have gone down to their graves,
And left me alone to my joys or my woes,
As a rock in the midst of the waves;

I am not old – I cannot be old,
Though tottering, wrinkled, and grey;
Though my eyes are dim, and my marrow is cold,
Call me not old to-day.

For, early memories round me throng,
Old times, and manners, and men,
As I look behind on my journey so long
Of threescore miles and ten.

I look behind, and am once more young,
Buoyant, and brave, and bold,
And my heart can sing, as of yore it sung,
Before they call'd me old.

I do not see her – the old wife there –
Shrivell'd, and haggard, and grey,
But I look on her blooming, and soft, and fair,
As she was on her wedding-day:

I do not see you, daughters and sons,
In the likeness of women and men,
But I kiss you now as I kissed you once,
My fond little children then:

And, as my own grandson rides on my knee
Or plays with his hoop or kite –
I can well recollect I was merry as he –
The bright-eyed little wight!

'Tis not long since – it cannot be long,
My years so soon were spent,
Since I was a boy, both straight and strong,
Yet now I am feeble and bent.

A dream, a dream – it is all a dream!
A strange, sad dream, good sooth;
For old as I am, and old as I seem,
My heart is full of youth:

Eye hath not seen, tongue hath not told,
And ear hath not heard it sung,
How buoyant and bold, though it seem to grow old,
Is the heart, for ever young:

For ever young – though life's old age
Hath every nerve unstrung;
The heart, the heart is a heritage
That keeps the old man young!

Martin Farquhar Tupper (1810–89)

≈ 299 ≈

Extract from A Game of Fives

Five little girls of Five, Four, Three, Two, One:
Rolling on the hearthrug, full of tricks and fun.

Five rosy girls, in years from Ten to Six:
Sitting down to lessons – no more time for tricks.

Five growing girls, from Fifteen to Eleven:
Music, Drawing, Languages, and food enough for seven!

Five winsome girls, from Twenty to Sixteen:
Each young man that calls, I say 'Now tell me which
    you mean!'

Five dashing girls, the youngest Twenty-one:
But, if nobody proposes, what is there to be done?

Five showy girls – but Thirty is an age
When girls may be engaging, but they somehow don't engage.

Five dressy girls, of Thirty-one or more:
So gracious to the shy young men they snubbed so
    much before!

Five passe girls – Their age? Well, never mind!
We jog along together, like the rest of human kind.

Lewis Carroll (1832–98)

A Mouthpiece

Why is the baby crying?
You must have scared or hit him.
'No, grandpa, I was trying
If your false teeth would fit him.'

John Bannister Tabb (1845–1909)

Life

Let me but live my life from year to year,
With forward face and unreluctant soul;
Not hurrying to, nor turning from the goal;
Not mourning for the things that disappear
In the dim past, nor holding back in fear
From what the future veils; but with a whole
And happy heart, that pays its toll
To Youth and Age, and travels on with cheer.

So let the way wind up the hill or down,
O'er rough or smooth, the journey will be joy:
Still seeking what I sought when but a boy,
New friendship, high adventure, and a crown,
My heart will keep the courage of the quest,
And hope the road's last turn will be the best.

Henry Van Dyke (1852–1933)

Time Is

Time is
Too Slow for those who Wait,
Too Swift for those who Fear,
Too Long for those who Grieve,
Too Short for those who Rejoice;
But for those who Love,
Time is not.

Henry Van Dyke (1852–1933)

She Was a Beauty

She was a beauty in the days
When Madison was President;
And quite coquettish in her ways –
On cardiac conquests much intent.

Grandpapa, on his right knee bent,
Wooed her in stiff, old-fashioned phrase – .
She was a beauty in the days
When Madison was President.

And when your roses where hers went
Shall go, my Lili, who date from Hayes,
I hope you'll wear her sweet content
Of whom tradition lightly says:
She was a beauty in the days
When Madison was President.

Henry Cuyler Bunner (1855–96)

Youth and Age

The last fruit off a tree is oft more sweet
And finely flavoured than the first, and so
Within life's autumn men may pleasures pluck
As sweet as youth's, and more sufficing than
The rank and rare enjoyments of the boy.

Robert Crawford (1868–1930)

Introducing the Day Family

Sun Day is a simple child,
   Face new washed and shining;
In the morning prim and mild –
   Church and mid-day dining.
If, before the shadows fall,
   You should find him going
Out to romp, or play at ball –
   Well, well. The child is growing.

Mon Day is a sulky boy.
   He frowns on work and hates it.
Tho' facing life should bring him joy,
   He ill appreciates it.
But Tues Day is a bright young man,
   Alert, well-dressed – oh, very –
Snatching pleasure where he can,
   Giving girls 'the merry.'

Wednes Day, stout and middle-aged,
   Seems hard-pressed and harried;
On grave affairs is he engaged;
   And very much he's married.
He holds severe and stubborn views –
   'Young folk, sir? Trouble breeders!'
He scans the day's financial news
   And always reads the leaders.

Thurs Day, tho' his hair be scant,
    Is bouyant, bland and jolly;
Tho' elderly, he's tolerant
    Of many a minor folly.
He owns a city business where
    He sits 'in consultation';
But all his grey-haired pals declare
    That golf's his occupation.

Old Fri Day grins a toothless grin –
    A grandfer, stooped and shrunken.
His chest, his cheeks are caving in,
    His dim old eyes deep sunken.
Yet, tho' he sit and moan and mope,
    All spent and worn with working,
Oft times a cunning gleam of hope
    In his old eyes seems lurking.

In Satur Day one might expect
    To find a wreck, fast dying.
Yet here's a lusty stripling decked
    For holiday, a-crying
To merry friends, in eager tones,
    All bound for playing spaces;
Or else his favourite he 'phones
    And takes her to the races.

C.J. Dennis (1876–1938)

Beautiful Old Age

It ought to be lovely to be old
to be full of the peace that comes of experience
and wrinkled ripe fulfilment.

The wrinkled smile of completeness that follows a life
lived undaunted and unsoured with accepted lies
they would ripen like apples, and be scented like pippins
in their old age.

Soothing, old people should be, like apples
when one is tired of love.
Fragrant like yellowing leaves, and dim with the soft
stillness and satisfaction of autumn.

And a girl should say:
It must be wonderful to live and grow old.
Look at my mother, how rich and still she is!

And a young man should think: By Jove
my father has faced all weathers, but it's been a life!

D.H. Lawrence (1885–1930)

Picture Credits

Index of Titles

Index of Poets